MW01243195

THE ENEMIES OFJOY

If you don't defend your joy, nobody will do it for you!

"The thief does not come except to steal, and to kill, and to destroy. I have come that they may have life, and that they may have it more abundantly".
John 10: 10. NKJV

JOSEPH BLESSING OMOSIGHO

THE ENEMIES OF JOY

Copyright © 2017 by: Joseph B. Omosigho
Written by: Joseph Blessing Omosigho
Cover designed by: Joseph Blessing Omosigho

Printed in the United States of America
Published by: Angels on Assignment, Inc.
Email: ministryofchrist@gmail.com
ISBN-13: 978-1546496069
ISBN-10: 1546496068

Dedication

This book is dedicated to all faithful children of God who are truly longing for more of God and less of themselves, with a strong desire to live a life FULL of joy and serve the Lord with gladness.

Also, dedicated to those who are willing to go all the way to combat and prevail over the enemies of joy, so with joy, they can fulfill the purpose for which God made them as salt of the earth and as the lights of the world for His glory, in Jesus name.

Acknowledgments

I do not take pride in writing this book. All the glory, praise, and honor belong to God Almighty, from whom all revelation, grace, and blessings flow. God just used me as a vessel to put this message together in a book for you and the body of Jesus Christ.

I thank my wife Gloria, and our children, David, Samuel, Hannah, and Moses, for their love, prayers, and support. I thank everyone the Lord has used, and is still using to help us in one way or another. Thank you all for your unrelenting, continued kindness and generosity. God will bless you, keep you in good health, and perfect all that concerns you, in Jesus' name, I pray. Amen!

I thank God for all my co-laborers and partners in the faith, for their continued love, prayers, passionate commitment, and dedication to our global mandate. I am truly humbled to be part of the team. You all make me complete in Him. Thank you.

It is my sincere prayer that your lives will be filled with unlimited joy, that the Almighty God will uproot the opposites of joy out of your lives and give you the grace to do what is written in the bible that will improve the levels of your joy from grace to grace and from glory to glory, in Jesus name.

Introduction

Any time you talk about Job in the Bible, you will be reminded how by God's grace he was able to combat the enemies of his joy, peace, and life. Job was successfully able to deal with the problems and difficulties in his life, finished well and strong to the glory of God. It was Job who stated in Job 14: 1, *"Man who is born of woman is of few days and full of trouble"*. I don't think you and I combined will have any joy left in us if all our children were to die in one day, if all our businesses/careers were lost in one day, if our homes/cars were burnt to the ground the same day; if all our hard-earned lifesavings/other investments were gone with the wind in one day, and then face humiliation, rejection, and the painful separation from our spouses too. The Bible said, in all this Job sinned not, nor did he blame God or others for his problems.

"Now there was a day when his sons and daughters were eating and drinking wine in their oldest brother's house; and a messenger came to Job and said, "The oxen were plowing and the donkeys feeding beside them, when the Sabeans raided them and took them away—indeed they have killed the servants with the edge of the sword; and I alone have escaped to tell you!" While he was still speaking, another also came and said, "The fire of God fell from heaven and burned up the sheep and the servants, and consumed them; and I alone have escaped to tell you!"

While he was still speaking, another also came and said, "The Chaldeans formed three bands, raided the camels and took them away, yes, and killed the servants with the edge of the sword; and I alone have escaped to tell you!" While he was still speaking, another also came and said, "Your sons and daughters were eating and drinking wine in their oldest brother's house, and suddenly a great wind came from across the wilderness and struck the four corners of the house, and it fell on the young people, and they are dead; and I alone have escaped to tell you!" Then Job arose, tore his robe, and shaved his head; and he fell to the ground and worshiped. And he said: "Naked I came from my mother's womb, and naked shall I return there. The Lord gave, and the Lord has taken away; Blessed be the name of the Lord." In all this, Job did not sin nor charge God with wrong". Job 1: 13-20 NKJV

Dealing with all the above in one week, Job did not commit suicide, he did not cry and did not complain, instead he was still able to praise and worship God. Job must have learned how to combat the enemies of joy, and thus was prepared to secure his joy no matter what came his way. How about you, do you know how to combat the enemies of your joy, are you prepared to secure your joy with everything you've got, or are you going to chicken out during life's challenges or difficulties; and leave your fate to chance?

This book was inspired by the Holy Spirit to help you and I get ready to defend, secure, and live our lives grounded in joy and peace. Don't forget, the devil is not dead yet, so his evil mission and mandate to steal, kill, and destroy is very much alive, he will do everything within his evil powers to shatter your joy. Please, I urge you by the mercies of God, to read this book prayerfully because I trust God by His Spirit will use this book to change your life and then use you to help others secure their joy. I pray God will help us overcome our enemies of joy, to be on the offensive against the opposite of joy, not on the defensive just merely existing or to settle for less, in Jesus name.

Table of Contents

Chapter 12

Chapter 1

What Is Joy?

The blessing of joy is the grace given to us by God to live in peace before, during, and after life's odds, challenges, or in normal times. Joy is the good feeling that empowers the soul in harmony with our human spirits when our connectivity with God is lively, often evident in the wellbeing of the body. Joy is the evidence of God's presence in our lives. If God is in your life, if you are filled with the Spirit of God, then this fruit of the Spirit—Joy, should be obvious in your life.

Joy is more than an ordinary good feeling, it is a matter of choice, powered by our decisions. God will never force joy on anybody, Joy is the product of a precious branch growing from the tree of life—*Jesus Christ*. God has given you and I the power to get the measure of joy we need from Him. The decisions you and I make daily have the potential to increase or hinder our joy. Joy, peace, grace, and love has been made available by God for us via the Holy Spirit through the redemptive work of Jesus. Joy is power, the strength to courageously persevere against all life's odds powered by our relationship and obedience to God. It is therefore up to you and I, to obey God and continue to enjoy unlimited joy, which the world cannot afford us by any means.

We Are Connected to Jesus

"I am the true Vine, and My Father is the vine-dresser. Every branch in Me that does not bear fruit, He takes away; and every branch that continues to bear fruit, He [repeatedly]
prunes, so that it will bear more fruit [even richer and finer fruit]. You are already clean because of the word which I have given you [the teachings which I have discussed with you]. Remain in Me, and I [will remain] in you. Just as no branch can

2

bear fruit by itself without remaining in the vine, neither can you [bear fruit, producing evidence of your faith] unless you remain in Me. I am the Vine; you are the branches. The one who remains in Me and I in him bears much fruit, for [otherwise] apart from Me [that is, cut off from vital union with Me] you can do nothing. If anyone does not remain in Me, he is thrown out like a [broken off] branch, and withers and dies; and they gather such branches and throw them into the fire, and they are burned.

If you remain in Me and My words remain in you [that is, if we are vitally united and My message lives in your heart], ask whatever you wish and it will be done for you. My Father is glorified and honored by this, when you bear much fruit, and prove yourselves to be My [true] disciples. I have loved you just as the Father has loved Me; remain in My love [and do not doubt My love for you]. If you keep My commandments and obey My teaching, you will remain in My love, just as I have kept My Father's commandments and remain in His love. I have told you these things so that My joy and delight may be in you, and that your joy may be made full and complete and overflowing." John 15: 1-11. AMP

Source of Joy

The source of joy is not of human origin, although we do have much to be joyful and thankful for, because we serve a good God who truly loves us. God is the source of our Joy. Humans like you and I can do good things that trigger, promote and propel joy, but only God can give joy. It is true that joy is a good feeling, but joy transcends beyond ordinary mere feeling or an emotional solace, it can elevate your spirit, empower your soul, and heal your body. The fact that joy is one of the fruits of the Spirit tells us that only God can help us bear such a life changing fruit. Thus, scripture tells us that the Kingdom of God is not all about food and drink, it is about righteousness, peace, and joy in the Holy Ghost.

*"[After all] the kingdom of God is not a matter of [getting the] food and drink [one likes], but **instead it is righteousness (that state which makes a person acceptable to God) and [heart] peace and joy in the Holy Spirit.**"*
Romans 14: 17. AMPC

Only God who have the ultimate power to fill you and I with joy. The things of this world will not fill any one with joy. It is very possible to be one of the richest people in the world and be lacking in joy, and it also very possible to be the poorest of all and be lacking in joy. In the same vein, it is possible to be very rich and be joyful, while it is also possible to be poor and still have joy. Joy is a matter of the heart, and only God can fill us with joy.

"May the God of your hope so fill you with all joy and peace in believing [through the experience of your faith] that by the power of the Holy Spirit you may abound and be overflowing (bubbling over) with hope". Romans 15: 13. AMPC

The Power of Joy Streams from God's Presence
The strength of our joy comes from drawing near to the Lord. The measure of our joy is proportioned to our nearness and to how much of God's presence we have in our lives. Simply put, the closer we are to Jesus, the stronger and the more joyous we become, He gives us a fresh supply of strength and joy daily. What the devil fears the most is God's presence. That is why Satan will try to do everything within his evil power to rob you of the Lord's presence. Joy cannot be bought from any physical or online stores, nor can any human like you and me give you joy. Joy can only be found in the presence of the Lord, not in materialism or money.

"Therefore, my heart is glad and my glory [my inner self] rejoices; my body too shall rest and confidently dwell in safety, You will show me the path of life; in Your presence is fullness of joy, at Your right hand there are pleasures forevermore".
Psalm 16: 9, 11. AMPC

4

Joy Flows from the Holy Spirit

The world's joy is temporary, conditionally based on the state of things or situational status. If things are going well, there is joy, when things are difficult, there is no joy. Our joy flows from the Spirit of God to us, and He will never run dry. His joy is ever fresh.

"The happiness [luxuriance; enjoyment] of evil people is brief, and the joy of the wicked [godless] lasts only a moment". Job 20: 2. EXB

Our joy as Christians comes from the Holy Spirit, He is the river of Joy, from which you and I get joy; He is the tree of life from which the fruits of joy are produced. If your joy as a Christian is situationally controlled or conditionally determined, you may need to reevaluate and audit your Christian life.

"And you became like us and like [imitators of us and of] the Lord. You suffered much [experienced many trials/much persecution], but still you accepted the teaching with the joy that comes from the Holy Spirit". 1 Thessalonians 1:6. EXB

Joy Is a Gift from God

"I perceived that there is nothing better for them than to be joyful and to do good as long as they live; also, that everyone should eat and drink and take pleasure in all his toil—this is God's gift to man". Ecclesiastes 3:12-13. ESV

Chapter 2

Some Other Words Related to Joy

There are other biblical words related to joy, that are often used too. Please find some of them below.

Happiness

Happiness is a good feeling which ranges from good promises, good fortune, situational based pleasure; temporal contentment to general good news for a season. We are often happy when things are going well harmoniously with our good plans, positive thoughts, and expectations. Happiness springs from what is going on around and within you—*health wise*. It is a state of metal consciousness which proceeds from the achievement of one's values, but can easily be depilated if things don't work out as planned. Happiness lacks the power to sustain us when failure, disappointment, and negativity hits us directly or indirectly. As Christians, God never promised us happiness, He only promised us joy. Happiness is earthly based but joy is eternal, joy will never die when we die or sleep physically, because heaven is full of joy. The main difference between happiness and joy is that; joy is a fruit of the Spirit and happiness is not. Joy is a life that flows from the tree of life—Jesus, to us and in us the more we abide in Him, and grow in His love. Happiness does not flow or grow from the tree of life.

"My soul has been cast far away from peace; I have forgotten happiness. So, I have seen that there is nothing better than that a man should be happy in his own works and activities, for that is his portion (share). For who will bring him [back] to see what will happen after he is gone? Though while he lives he counts himself happy and prosperous—and though people praise you when you do well for yourself—a man [who is held] in honor, yet who lacks [spiritual] understanding and a

teachable heart, is like the beasts that perish". Lamentations 3:17; Ecclesiastes 3:22; Psalm 49:18, 20. AMP

Delight

Delight is a higher level of happiness. It means to take pleasure in a person or a thing. Delight comes from the enjoyment of a thing. Delight also comes from a good relationship, the benefit of, the presence of, or on behalf of, a good and kind person. Some people take delight in what is good and some people take delight in what is evil/wrong. Many people nowadays delight themselves in their educational or social status; material possessions or political might, and other temporary fun things of this world, which never satisfies. What satisfies the void in our souls is Jesus and the joy He gives, when we delight ourselves in Him. To delight oneself in the Lord is to trust, rely on Him, and to continue to do those things that please God like Jesus did during His earthly ministry.

"So, Jesus said, "When you lift up the Son of Man [on the cross], you will know then [without any doubt] that I am He, and that I do nothing on My own authority, but I say these things just as My Father taught Me. And He who sent Me is [always] with Me; He has not left Me alone, because I always do what pleases Him. Trust [rely on and have confidence] in the Lord and do good; dwell in the land and feed [securely] on His faithfulness. Delight yourself in the Lord, and He will give you the desires and petitions of your heart. Commit your way to the Lord; trust in Him also and He will do it". Psalm 37: 3-5; John 8: 28-29. AMP

Gladness

Gladness is another word often interchanged with the word joy. Gladness is a pleasurable state of being trilled, an amusement, and personal satisfaction either on how things are going, on one's achievements and success or accomplishment. It is a blessing to be saved, but it takes the grace of God to be able to serve the Lord with gladness during persecution, trials, and temptations.

"Serve the Lord with gladness and delight; Come before His presence with joyful singing. For the Lord, will comfort Zion [in her captivity]; He will comfort all her ruins. And He will make her wilderness like Eden, and her desert like the garden of the Lord; Joy and gladness will be found in her, Thanksgiving and the voice of a melody. So, the redeemed of the Lord will return and come with joyful shouting to Zion; Everlasting joy will be on their heads. They will obtain gladness and joy, and sorrow and sighing will flee away". Psalm 100:2;
Isaiah 51:3, 11. AMP

Cheerfulness

Cheerfulness is more of how happiness and gladness is expressed, because one may be able to conceal happiness, but it is very difficult to conceal a heart that is cheerful. Cheerfulness is like when a light comes on after one has been in the dark for too long.

"A heart full of joy and goodness makes a cheerful face, but when a heart is full of sadness the spirit is crushed. Go your way, eat your bread with joy and drink your wine with a cheerful heart [if you are righteous, wise, and in the hands of God]; for God, has already approved and accepted your works. Let your clothes always be white [with purity], and do not let the oil [of gladness] be lacking on your head". Proverbs 15:13;
Ecclesiastes 9:7-8. AMP

Jesus was well known to encourage people to be of good cheer. I encourage you to be of good cheer. Learn to rest in, rely on, and cast all your cares, life's issues, and challenges on the Lord, and He will take care of you. Please don't give up on God, He will not give up on you. Raise your head up, stand up straight, and be that person God created you to be for His glory. Don't allow any situation or anyone to hinder you from shining for the Lord as the light of the world. You are the salt of the earth, don't allow anybody to stop you from allowing the world to taste and see the goodness of God in your life. You must not

8

settle for less, be of good cheer, you are the son or daughter of the king of glory, go into all the world and shine as light. Stop allowing the devil to steal, kill and destroy your joy. Cheer up, go light the world for Jesus Christ with joy as you serve the Lord with gladness and cheerfulness. This is your day, it is the day the Lord has made for you, rejoice and be glad in it.

"Then behold, they brought to Him a paralytic lying on a bed. When Jesus saw their faith, He said to the paralytic, "Son, be of good cheer; your sins are forgiven you." But Jesus turned around, and when He saw her He said, "Be of good cheer, daughter; your faith has made you well." And the woman was made well from that hour. But immediately Jesus spoke to them, saying, "Be of good cheer! It is I; do not be afraid".
Matthew 9:2, 22; 14: 27. NKJV

Rejoice or Rejoicing

It saddens my heart to note that some Christians nowadays only rejoice when they see or experience a miracle, the manifestation of the gifts of the Spirit or when good things come their way. God expects you and I to rejoice always, because only the living can praise Him. We rejoice in the Lord because we love Him, not just because of what He has done for us, or the good things He promised to do for us. If our joy is based on things, needs, and wants, what will happen when those things, needs, and wants are met?

"Love endures with patience and serenity, love is kind and thoughtful, and is not jealous or envious; love does not brag and is not proud or arrogant. It is not rude; it is not self-seeking, it is not provoked [nor overly sensitive and easily angered]; it does not take into account a wrong endured. It does not rejoice at injustice, but rejoices with the truth [when right and truth prevail]. Finally, believers, rejoice! Be made complete [be what you should be], be comforted, be like-minded, live in peace [enjoy the spiritual well-being experienced by believers who walk closely with God]; and the God of love and peace [the source of lovingkindness] will be with you".
1 Corinthians 13:4-6; 2 Corinthians 13:11. AMP

Chapter 3

The Enemies of Joy (Part 1)

The enemies of joy don't care who you are, they are on a mission to frustrate, demoralize, and truncate your joy any way they can, if you don't take adequate steps to defend yourself, defeat them, and secure your joy. If you don't defend your joy, nobody else will do it for you. Joy has a lot of enemies, some of them are:

Sin Is the Number One Enemy of Joy

One of the dangers of sin is the betrayer of God's love, taking for granted the sacrifice of Jesus's sufferings and death for us on the Cross of Calvary. Non-Christians may appear to enjoy sin, but really, they don't, because the payment for sin is death. Christians ought not to be so, we ought to be different because we are a new breed, birthed by Jesus Christ through His shed blood. Any Christian who enjoys sinning is really a pretender, who is yet to be broken by the hammer of God's word, because he or she cannot be like Christ walking and living like worldly people. Sin gradually eats up joy like the soldier ants eats up big and mighty trees from their roots. When those soldier ants really mean business, it does not matter whether the tree is small or big, it may take a long time, but it will eventually come down.

Any sin has the potential to kill joy like little foxes that spoils the vine. Sin spoils our communion with Christ, cuts off our daily supply of joy, and can limit our intimacy with God, the source of our joy. The apostle Paul made it very clear that sin has consequences. If you make others unhappy or mess up their joy, your happiness and joy will be messed up too in due time, because whatever you sow, you will reap. If you sow joy, you will reap joy, if you sow evil, evil you will reap. Don't forget, you will be treated someday, just how you are treating others now directly or indirectly.

"Do not be deceived, God is not mocked [He will not allow Himself to be ridiculed, nor treated with contempt nor allow His precepts to be scornfully set aside]; for whatever a man sows, this and this only is what he will reap. For the one who sows to his flesh [his sinful capacity, his worldliness, his disgraceful impulses] will reap from the flesh ruin and destruction, but the one who sows to the Spirit will from the Spirit reap eternal life. Let us not grow weary or become discouraged in doing good, for at the proper time we will reap, if we do not give in". Galatians 6: 7-9. AMP

Haters

Haters do only one thing best in their lives, they hate. They hate to see others prosper, succeed, happy, or joyful. It is very sad to note that a lot of ministry leaders are guilty of hate, by lying and deceiving God's people because of the love of money, fame, and earthly influence. If you are close to, related to, or work with any hater, it will be very difficult for you to maintain your joy in their presence. They take pleasure in, and enjoy making life difficult for others. A good example of a hater is a terrorist who will stop at nothing to destroy other people lives, hence they don't care about losing his or her own life.

"I said, "Listen, you leaders of Israel! You are supposed to know right from wrong, but you are the very ones who hate good and love evil. You skin my people alive and tear the flesh from their bones. Yes, you eat my people's flesh, strip off their skin, and break their bones. You chop them up like meat for the cooking pot". Micah 3: 1-3. NLT

Haters Are Joy Stealers

What haters enjoy doing is to cause trouble and propagate gossip with a passion to steal, kill, and destroy other people's joy and peace. God warns you and I not to be haters ourselves. You are a hater, if you are acting/behaving as the enemy of joy to others. God in His word encourages us as Christians to be strong in the Lord, and in the power of His might, if we must overcome the wiles of the devil, because we are in the last days.

Many nowadays only care about the money they make, not the lives they take or mess up for them to make the money. Anyone who gets on their way, they will take out in a heartbeat, it doesn't matter who you are, except God intervenes. Be ready to do everything you can to defend and secure your joy because the last days are here. A lot of terrible things are happening around us that will try to limit our joy if we are not able to process or handle them well.

"You should know this, Timothy, that in the last days there will be very difficult times. For people, will love only themselves and their money. They will be boastful and proud, scoffing at God, disobedient to their parents, and ungrateful. They will consider nothing sacred. They will be unloving and unforgiving; they will slander others and have no self-control. They will be cruel and hate what is good. They will betray their friends, be reckless, be puffed up with pride, and love pleasure rather than God. They will act religious, but they will reject the power that could make them godly. Stay away from people like that!" 2 Timothy 3: 1-5. NLT

Unfriendly Friends

The most dangerous people to deal with in life are unfriendly friends, you don't know who they are but they know you very well. They are often satanic agents on a mission to kill, steal, and destroy for Satan directly or indirectly. They pretend to love, care, and are willing to help, when in fact they are the enemies of your destiny, joy, and peace. When you choose who to make your friend, please don't take it for granted, because your life, success, and failure could depend on that person. Judas Iscariot, one of Jesus's disciples was the one who betrayed Him with a kiss. So, please my dear, prayerfully choose your friends. Unfriendly friends are expert manipulators, they are wolves in sheep's clothing.

"For it is not an enemy who reproaches and taunts me—then I might bear it; nor is it one who has hated me who insolently vaunts himself against me—then I might hide from him.

But it was you, a man my equal, my companion and my familiar friend. We had sweet fellowship together and used to walk to the house of God in company". Psalm 55:12-14. AMPC

Some church leaders are unfriendly friends, satanic workers in sheep's clothing. Many false leaders, prophets, and pastors are operating from the sea, graveyards, and from satanic altars. Please be very careful who you call your pastor/leader and who you allow to lay hands on your precious head. If you want to know more about fake leaders/prophets/pastors, please get a copy of my book, "Pastor' and Church Leader' Con Games".

"But there were false teachers among the people. And there will be false teachers among you also. These people will work in secret ways to bring false teaching to you. They will turn against Christ Who bought them with His blood. They bring fast death on themselves. Many people will follow their wrong ways. Because of what they do, people will speak bad things against the way of truth. They will tell lies and false stories so they can use you to get things for themselves. But God judged them long ago and their death is on the way.

Then the Word of the Lord came to me saying, "Son of man, speak against those of Israel who speak false words in My name. Say to those who tell what is going to happen in the future out of their own minds, 'Listen to the Word of the Lord! The Lord God says, "It is bad for the foolish people who tell what is going to happen by following their own spirit and have seen nothing. O Israel, your men who speak in My name are of no more worth than foxes in destroyed cities. You have not gone up to the broken places to build the wall around the people of Israel so that it will stand in the battle on the day of the Lord.

They have lied and have spoken false words using their secret ways, saying, 'This is what the Lord says,' when the Lord has not sent them. Yet they hope that what they say will come

*true. Did you not see a false dream and tell a lie using your
secret ways when you said, 'This is what the Lord says,' when
I have not spoken?" So, the Lord God says: "Because you have
spoken false words and seen a lie, I am against you," says the
Lord God. "My hand will be against those who see false dreams
and speak false words. They will have no place in the gathering
of My wise people. Their names will not be written down with
the people of Israel. And they will not go into the land of Israel.
Then you will know that I am the Lord God".*
2 Peter 2: 1-3; Ezekiel 13: 1-9. NLV

Satanic Agents

Satanic agents are more dangerous then Satan himself, because they are God made instruments the devil has subverted
through deception, and now uses against fellow humans, anything that glorifies God and God children. Satan cannot stand
against God but He can stand in the presence of God once he is
housed by humanity, thereby using humanity as a vehicle or
shield. Real satanic agents don't really have to befriend you to
harm you. They are hardcore haters whose brains have been
cooked in wickedness, and their hearts sealed with hot iron of
evil passion. It doesn't matter whether you are their child,
spouse, friend or neighbor, whoever the devil or his evil leaders
order them to harm they will hurt without compromise. They
can use anything, any means to frustrate and destroy your joy,
ranging from false dreams, false accusations or betrayal by
loved ones. Sometimes, they will place big loads of obstacles
and problems on your way to success physically or spiritually,
just to kill your joy.

Jesus Christ Himself made it very clear that the devil has
his own children on earth, just as we are called the children of
God. On the record, there are churches of Satan in some coun-
tries now, and they are spreading in America very well. On their
websites, they state that their mission is to promote sin and win
souls for the devil. Muslims leaders are now conducting praise
worship, and worship on Sunday mornings as we do, in order

to get more converts. They try to make people happy temporally by providing for their basic needs to get them converted to Islam especially in African and other undeveloped areas of the world.

"You are of your father, the devil, and it is your will to practice the lusts and gratify the desires [which are characteristic] of your father. He was a murderer from the beginning and does not stand in the truth, because there is no truth in him. When he speaks a falsehood, he speaks what is natural to him, for he is a liar [himself] and the father of lies and of all that is false". John 8: 44. AMPC

Satan

I don't have to remind you that the devil and his evil spirits are your enemies of joy, you already know, because we do not fight against flesh and blood, but the devil/evil spirits who wants to kill, steal and destroy our joy, peace, and lives.

"[For] Our fight [conflict; struggle] is not against people on earth [flesh and blood] but against the rulers and authorities and the powers [or cosmic powers/rulers] of this world's darkness [darkness], against the spiritual powers of evil in the heavenly world [realm; places]". Ephesians 6:12. EXB

You Can Be Your Own Enemy of Joy

There is no doubt that you and I can be our own enemies of joy, because we sometimes give the devil the ammunition to use against us. Below you will find some of the ways we can become our own enemies of joy.

1. **Careless Words**: We can recreate our worlds for good or bad. Life and death are in the power of our tongues.
2. **Careless Spending:** You cannot eat your cake and have it too. There is nothing good or pretty about being in the bondage of debt. A borrower will always be a slave to the lender.
3. **Careless Decisions:** Our decisions can make or break us. One bad decision can cause the pain of a lifetime.

4. **Careless investment**: I learned this vital life lesson in a very hard and bad way. When poverty and debt comes knocking at the door of your life, shame and reproach are not far away.

5. **Laziness:** It is a disease and leads to temptation of criminal intentions. Laziness has made many people fall for evil attractions and to embrace criminality as a profession.

6. **Selfishness:** It is the mother of all sins, it gave birth to greed, pride, and strife. Selfishness is married to lust and together they can turn a beautiful home into a home of pain, bitterness, and shame.

7. **Walking in the flesh:** When you walk in the flesh, you will reap the fruits of the flesh. Sometimes we place great value on things (gold, diamonds, and silver), and animals (pets); more than we do fellow humans who are under privileged.

8. **Corruption:** It is the love of money, materialism and fame, together they constitute the tree of all evil. The tree of corruption is planted on the soil of greed, lust, and pride.

9. **Curses**: Curses are powerful instruments of destruction; a cursed person will not have joy until the curse is broken. A curse can turn a king into a slave in due time.

10. **Evil covenants**: Evil covenants can be deadly in nature and by design. Any evil agreement is in part a partnership with the devil directly or indirectly, and will always impair joy.

11. **When you place yourself first and God last in your life:** You cannot live on your own without the life God has given you. When you put God last, your life automatically begins to work in reverse, and against the divine order of life.

12. **Lack of integrity:** It will be impossible for you to go far in life if nobody can trust you. They may follow you

and pretend to love you because of what you have, but not for very long. It is better to be poor and rich in integrity, than to be rich and build mansions on the foundation of lies. When the wind of truth and justice blows, the poor with integrity have the hope of becoming rich, but the rich whose foundation is lies will start sinking. Don't forget that the devil is the father and inventor of lies, liars draw their strength from him. He has no joy, neither will he allow you to have joy in your own life if you embrace the lifestyle of lying.

Chapter 4

The Enemies of Joy (Part 2)

Since the joy of the Lord is our strength. Targeting our joy is the main or major focus of our enemies—the devil and his evil hosts/agents to attack strength. The number one enemy of joy is not the devil, it is our disobedience to God. When we obey God, the devil becomes powerless, because God will fight for us. The devil can fight you and I to try to get at God through us, but he can never dare to put up a fight with the Almighty God directly. Disobedience is in three degrees. First; refusing to obey (an intentional choice). Secondly: Failing to obey (could be circumstantial reasons or due to direct or indirect excuses). Thirdly: Half obedience (selfishness, complacency, or satanic attack in the form of carelessness or distraction). Either way, God does not tolerate disobedience in any form or way, thus each disobedience has consequences attached to it. Unless there is sincere repentance based on Jesus' sacrifice of love through His shed blood, your joy will soon start to dry up. On the other hand, blessings, joy, and promotion are attached to obedience.

"Therefore, because of you [that is, your sin and disobedience] the heavens withhold the dew and the earth withholds its produce." Now it shall be, if you diligently listen to and obey the voice of the Lord your God, being careful to do all of His commandments which I am commanding you today, the Lord your God will set you high above all the nations of the earth. All these blessings will come upon you and overtake you if you pay attention to the voice of the Lord your God.

"You will be blessed in the city, and you will be blessed in the field. "The offspring of your body and the produce of your ground and the offspring of your animals, the offspring of your herd and the young of your flock will be blessed. "Your basket and your kneading bowl will be blessed. "You will be blessed when you come in and you will be blessed when you go out.

18

"The Lord will cause the enemies who rise up against you to be defeated before you; they will come out against you one way, but flee before you seven ways. The Lord will command the blessing upon you in your storehouses and in all that you undertake, and He will bless you in the land which the Lord your God gives you"". Haggi 1: 10; Deuteronomy 28:1-8. AMP

Disobedience Makes Room for Fear

Disobedience eats up our joy, impedes our boldness, and makes room for shame and fear. The devil then takes advantage of the legal ground we give him to come in to steal, kill, and destroy.

"Therefore, since [these His] children share in flesh and blood [the physical nature of mankind], He Himself in a similar manner also shared in the same [physical nature, but without sin], so that through [experiencing] death He might make powerless (ineffective, impotent) him who had the power of death—that is, the devil, and [that He] might free all those who through [the haunting] fear of death were held in slavery throughout their lives. The fear of man brings a snare, but whoever trusts in and puts his confidence in the Lord will be exalted and safe". Hebrews 2:14-15; Proverbs 29:25. AMP

The Spirit of Offense

Another deadly evil spirit the devil has empowered, and given a specific mandate to target our joy with precision is called the spirit of offense. You and I cannot stop offenses from coming to us, because we only have the capacity to control what we do and not what others do. There is nothing pretty about offense, whether small or big, its power can truncate, destabilize our joy, and invoke disaster and crisis of all kinds. Jesus Christ our Lord warned us ahead of time that offenses will certainly come.

"He (Jesus) said to His disciples, "Offenses will certainly come, but woe to the one they come through! It would be better for him if a millstone were hung around his neck and he were

thrown into the sea than for him to cause one of these little ones to stumble". Luke 17: 1-2. HCSB (Jesus added)

Any time offenses occur, it often opens the doors to other enemies of joy. As Christians, how we react to offenses can either increase or decrease our level of joy. Please understand that we are all different and unique individuals, we see things differently, process things our own ways, and react/respond to incidents/situations or circumstances uniquely. What may offend me may not offend you, and what you may overlook I may consider very offensive and bad. Sometimes our cultural backgrounds, up-bringing, enlightenment, exposure/education, and ignorance are the reasons behind our view of things. In the Christian faith, unbroken Christians are more vulnerable to offense than mature Christians, while mature Christians are not innocent, hence they too can be caught off guard by the spirit of offense. Offenses range from a mere misunderstanding to murmuring or grumbling, anger (all levels of anger), bitterness; hatred and unforgiveness, to mention a few. Time will not permit us to cover all the above, we will concern ourselves with murmuring and grumbling; anger, bitterness, and unforgiveness, hence we already covered haters in the enemies of joy part one.

Murmuring and Grumbling

Miriam and Aaron murmured and grumbled against Moses, the man of God, and God's anger was unleashed, Miriam the instigator become leprous. Miriam's joy was taken away. Any time you come under attack by the spirit of murmuring and grumbling, please resist them and don't give them any room or allow them to use you. If you give them a place or allow them to use you, your joy will be attacked, limited, killed, or stolen from you.

"Now Miriam and Aaron spoke against Moses because of the Cushite woman whom he had married (for he had married a Cushite woman); and they said, "Has the Lord really spoken only through Moses? Has He not spoken also through us?" And the Lord heard it. And the anger of the Lord was kindled

against Miriam and Aaron, and He departed. But when the cloud had withdrawn from over the tent, behold, Miriam was leprous, as white as snow. And Aaron turned and looked at Miriam, and, behold, she was leprous. Then Aaron said to Moses, "Oh, my lord, I plead with you, do not account this sin to us, in which we have acted foolishly and in which we have sinned." Numbers 12: 1-2, 9-11. AMP

Bitterness

No Christian wants to be a bitter Christian, but we cannot control what others do, sometimes things happen directly or indirectly to us, or to our loved ones that makes bitterness sneak in on us. Bitterness is a spiritual poison, which often leads to physical problems. Bitterness is like a viper, it often starts in the form of anger, its venom can be deadly. Some people tend to conceal their bitterness with a fake or false smile on the outside, but on the inside, they declare war. It is at this point that evil spirits take over, feeding on our negative emotions against others, using the negative circumstances around us, which often leads to spiritual bondage, because demons thrive in any environment where there is bitterness.

"Look after each other so that none of you fails to receive the grace of God. Watch out that no poisonous root of bitterness grows up to trouble you, corrupting many".
Hebrews 12:15. NLT

Bottling up Bitterness, Can Bottle up Your Joy

The more we hold onto anger and bitterness, the devil uses our past, pain, and negative experiences to steal, kill, or destroy our joy. Please stop bottling up bitterness in your heart, because it is your joy you are bottling up. Let go, and you will be free to enjoy your freedom in Christ. Don't allow bitterness to poison your joy any more, let it go and let God—Joy into your life, in Jesus name. Stop allowing bitterness to trouble your life, because any time you bottle up bitterness, you indirectly or directly bottle up your joy too.

"And do not give the devil an opportunity [to lead you into sin by holding a grudge, or nurturing anger, or harboring resentment, or cultivating bitterness]. Let all bitterness and wrath and anger and clamor [perpetual animosity, resentment, strife, fault-finding] and slander be put away from you, along with every kind of malice [all spitefulness, verbal abuse, malevolence]. Be kind and helpful to one another, tender-hearted [compassionate, understanding], forgiving one another [readily and freely], just as God in Christ also forgave you".
Ephesians 4:27, 31-32. AMP

Anger

Anger is often the foothold that leads to the stronghold of bitterness. Anger by itself has the capacity to operate on its own prowess as a standalone problem, ranging from a mere quarrel to destructive—satanic anger. One thing you and I must understand is that, offense will come, some of which is meant to surface in us, and sometimes it is satanic attack. Jesus' stance on the issue of anger is very clear. Therefore, as Christians, we must rely on God's grace to overcome the temptation to become angry, because most of the time, anger leads to sin if not placed in check right away. The book of proverbs declared that negative anger is a foolish act. It is my prayer that you and I will not become fools, or act like one by becoming angry, or by sinning against God and mankind, in Jesus name.

"For I am afraid that perhaps when I come I may find you not to be as I wish, and that you may find me not as you wish— that perhaps there may be strife, jealousy, angry tempers, disputes, slander, gossip, arrogance and disorder. A [shortsighted] fool always loses his temper and displays his anger, but a wise man [uses self-control and] holds it back".
2 Corinthians 12:20; Proverbs 29:11. AMP

Unforgiveness

Any heart engulfed with unforgiveness is like a grave that is full of dead men's bones and such a heart is never satisfied, always actively searching for more faults and mistakes to justify its deadly quest. Unforgiveness is fueled by excuses, pride, and greed. Such excuses are fueled by the devil, the accuser of Christians. Pride is Satan's finest and classic tool of destruction ranking second to sin—Lust. Greed is lust bound by the yoke of selfishness, spiced with the deceitfulness of pride. Jesus understood the deadly impact of unforgiveness, and thus warned us to stay away from unforgiveness. Jesus even went as far as giving us an order to forgive to help us, so we don't have any excuse. Now, if you are a Christian, and if Jesus Christ is really your master, Lord, and savior, if you fail to forgive those who offended you, you cannot be a part of Him completely yet, because you are still walking in disobedience. God said forgive, it is not a suggestion or an opinion, it is an order. If you want God to always hear your prayers, you MUST learn to always forgive.

"Whenever you stand praying, if you have anything against anyone, forgive him [drop the issue, let it go], so that your Father who is in heaven will also forgive you your transgressions and wrong doings [against Him and others]. Then Peter came to Him and asked, "Lord, how many times will my brother sin against me and I forgive him and let it go? Up to seven times?" Jesus answered him, "I say to you, not up to seven times, but seventy times seven.

"Therefore, the kingdom of heaven is like a king who wished to settle accounts with his slaves. When he began the accounting, one who owed him 10,000 talents was brought to him. "But because he could not repay, his master ordered him to be sold, with his wife and his children and everything that he possessed, and payment to be made. So, the slave fell on his knees and begged him, saying, 'Have patience with me and I will repay you everything.' And his master's heart was moved with compassion and he released him and forgave him [canceling] the debt. But that same slave went out and found one of his fellow slaves who owed him a hundred denarii; and he seized him and began choking him, saying, 'Pay what you owe!'

So, his fellow slave fell on his knees and begged him earnestly, 'Have patience with me and I will repay you.' But he was unwilling and he went and had him thrown in prison until he paid back the debt. When his fellow slaves saw what had happened, they were deeply grieved and they went and reported to their master [with clarity and in detail] everything that had taken place. Then his master called him and said to him, 'You wicked and contemptible slave, I forgave all that [great] debt of yours because you begged me. Should you not have had mercy on your fellow slave [who owed you little by comparison], as I had mercy on you?' And in wrath his master turned him over to the torturers (jailers) until he paid all that he owed". Mark 11: 25; Matthew 18:21-34. AMP

Chapter 5

The Opposites of Joy

Joy has many opposites, negatives that have the capacity to frustrate, truncate, and destroy your joy if you don't declare war on them until you completely overcome them by the grace of God.

Shame

Shame is a very bad emotional feeling that arises from the consciousness or awareness that something is wrong with you, or when something bad has happened that you feel was not supposed to happen. Shame could be about yourself, or someone or something that is associated to you directly or indirectly. For example, when failure occurs, when expectations are high or not high, and when we feel we have let ourselves or others down. When something dishonorable happens, or an improper act or ridiculous miss-behavior from or by somebody we care about in public places. Shame for the most part does not always operate alone; its powerful teammates include embarrassment and disgrace. Shame is as old as humanity, hence the first man and woman, Adam and Eve felt ashamed after they betrayed God's love and kindness by disobeying Him. There is nothing nice about shame. Shame is a reproach that has led many to premature deaths, while many others are committing slow suicide, shame is eating them up on the inside. Shame kills joy.

"Since the days of our fathers to this day we have been exceedingly guilty; and on account of our wrongdoings we, our kings, and our priests have been handed over to the kings of the lands, to the sword, to captivity, to plundering, and to complete shame, as it is today". Ezra 9:7. AMP

As Christians, we must not allow ourselves to be overcome by shame or allow shame to consume our joy with the fire of embarrassment and disgrace. If you give place to shame it will break your heart and dash your joy into pieces. David cried out and said in Psalm 69: 20. AMP; *"Reproach and insults have broken my heart and I am so sick. I looked for sympathy, but there was none, and for comforters, but I found none".*

You may be perfect, but I know I am not, nor does God expect me to be by my own power and might, that is why Jesus died and grace was released through the Holy Spirit to help me become complete (perfect) through the righteousness of Jesus Christ. You must not be ashamed of your past, you have been washed by the shed blood of Jesus Christ, and you must never be ashamed to be a Christian or of the gospel of Christ.

"I am not ashamed of the gospel, for it is the power of God for salvation [from His wrath and punishment] to everyone who believes [in Christ as Savior], to the Jew first and also to the Greek. "Do not fear, for you will not be put to shame, and do not feel humiliated or ashamed, for you will not be disgraced. For you will forget the shame of your youth, and you will no longer remember the disgrace of your widowhood. Instead of your [former] shame you will have a double portion; And instead of humiliation your people will shout for joy over their portion. Therefore, in their land they will possess double [what they had forfeited]; Everlasting joy will be theirs".
Romans 1: 16; Isaiah 54: 4; 61: 7. AMP

We All Have Our Own Past

The beauty of success is its history of challenges, battles, and victories. Any success without a story of challenges overcome is a product of manipulation or sin, unless if it was inherited. Whatever you did or who you were before you became born again must not rid you of your joy, please let it go, and let God move you forward. Let your past be gone with the wind, focus on the present, and prayerfully prepare for your future; for the end of a thing is better than its beginning. Today is a new day, you are a new person, so let old things pass away, and make room for God to do new things in your life. Jesus Christ has set you free and you are free indeed.

It is my own eager expectation and hope, that [looking toward the future] I will not disgrace myself nor be ashamed in anything, but that with courage and the utmost freedom of speech, even now as always, Christ will be magnified and exalted in my body, whether by life or by death. For to me, to live is Christ [He is my source of joy, my reason to live] and to die is gain [for I will be with Him in eternity]. Therefore, if anyone is in Christ [that is, grafted in, joined to Him by faith in Him as Savior], he is a new creature [reborn and renewed by the Holy Spirit]; the old things [the previous moral and spiritual condition] have passed away. Behold, new things have come [because spiritual awakening brings a new life]".
Philippians 1:20-21; 2 Corinthians 5:17. AMP

Sorrow

Sorrow is a sad feeling or pain of deep distress caused by loss, continued disappointment, or other life's misfortunes suffered by oneself, or the people you love or care about. Sorrow and grief often go together. None of us are immune to sorrow, each one of us cannot escape times of grief and sorrow at some point in life. Being a Christian does not insulate you from tragedies or painful situations, but it does guarantee you that the Holy Spirit will always provide you the comfort and solace you need during and after such times. Thus, we don't weep, sorrow, or grief as the world does.

Some Christians believe that once you are saved, you are sorrow free, yes you are free in the spirit, but you still live on earth, where fake Christians, terrorism, and wicked people are on the rise. The Christian life is a race, a battlefield, and a glorious one too. If you run the race by the book (Bible), you will not be disqualified. If you fight the good fight of faith and win by being faithful to the end, you will receive the crown of glory. After you receive the crown of glory, the rest of your life all eternity will know no sorrow forever, you will rest in peace, enjoy glory, and forever abide in glory to part no more.

28

Job's Biblical Way of Dealing with Sorrow

There is no better example of how to find hope in times of sorrow than Job in the Bible. Job fought the spirit of sorrow one on one. One of the most overwhelming challenges during severe trial or sorrow is often time the question "Why"? Job did not question God's grace or love toward him. He knew that God knew and understood what he was going through.

Job Knew God Was Aware of His Situation

Job did not run away from God, he ran into God for help in times of sorrow and trouble. Job accepted his sorrow and knew God was in control if he was living right with God. The question to you my friend is this; are you living right with God or are you using God like a vending machine that you only go to when you are in need? Job kept his relationship with God intact. How is your relationship with God?

"But he knows where I am and what I've done. He can cross-examine me all He wants, and I'll pass the test with honors. I've followed Him closely, my feet in His footprints, not once swerving from His way. I've obeyed every word He's spoken, and not just obeyed His advice—I've treasured it.
Job 23:10-12. MSG

Job praised God during his sorrow. Some of us only praise God when we get the victory, not Job, he knew God too well to doubt His faithfulness. Job was praising God in advance, trusting God to turn his pain to gain. Some us complain instead of praying, forgetting that God will never respond to our complains, He only responds to our prayers of faith.

Even if He kills me, I will hope in Him. I will still defend my ways before Him. Yes, this will result in my deliverance, for no godless person can appear before Him". Job 13:15-16. HCSB

Job Maintained His Integrity and Refused to Quit

"Job continued his discourse, saying: As God lives, who has deprived me of justice, and the Almighty who has made me bitter, as long as my breath is still in me and the breath from

*God remains in my nostrils, my lips will not speak unjustly,
and my tongue will not utter deceit. I will never affirm that you
are right. I will maintain my integrity until I die. I will cling to
my righteousness and never let it go. My conscience will not
accuse me as long as I live!"* Job 27: 1-6. HCSB

In Case of Loss, Take Heart

*"We do not want you to be uninformed, brothers, concern-
ing those who are asleep, so that you will not grieve like the
rest, who have no hope. Since we believe that Jesus died and
rose again, in the same way God will bring with Him those who
have fallen asleep through Jesus. For we say this to you by a
revelation from the Lord: We who are still alive at the Lord's
coming will certainly have no advantage over those who have
fallen asleep. For the Lord Himself will descend from heaven
with a shout, with the archangel's voice, and with the trumpet
of God, and the dead in Christ will rise first. Then we who are
still alive will be caught up together with them in the clouds to
meet the Lord in the air and so we will always be with the
Lord. Therefore encourage one another with these words".*
1 Thessalonians 4: 13-18. HCSB

Please don't allow sorrow to consume your joy, make you
bitter or burned out; rather let God use the situation to make you
better and brighter, in Jesus name! He knows best, when He
allows something to happen, it is always for a reason. Though
we don't often agree with his choices or decision to allow our
loved one to depart, but we can always trust Him that He knows
what He is doing because He loves us and His love toward us
is never for bad, but for good.

Troubled

We all deal with trouble from time to time, if you don't go
looking for trouble, sometimes trouble will come looking for
you through trials, temptation, persecution, and satanic attacks.
The devil will stop at nothing to block the flow of your joy, he

will gladly open the doors of sadness, depression, misery, calamity, and dejection with some fancy worldly attractions or use materialism as a bate to lure you into his net. It is almost practically impossible to not worry during troubling situations or circumstances. Nevertheless, Jesus Christ is always standing by with open arms asking us to come to Him for help.

"Come to Me, all who are weary and heavily burdened [by religious rituals that provide no peace], and I will give you rest [refreshing your souls with salvation]. Take My yoke upon you and learn from Me [following Me as My disciple], for I am gentle and humble in heart, and you will find rest (renewal, blessed quiet) for your souls". Matthew 11: 28-29. AMP

Jesus Said Trouble Will Come and Assured Us Victory

Jesus never asked us to go looking for trouble, if trouble comes to us, we have the right to defend ourselves wisely as serpents and harmless as doves. Moreover, He said God has given us the power to get the victory, because He has overcome the world. Don't fear trouble, wisely stand your ground when trouble comes. Resist trouble per the capacity of your faith, and flee if need be without shame, so you can be alive to fight again another day as led by the Spirit of God. Even Jesus waited for His time, don't be unwise and die before your time. There is time for everything. Be wise!

"I have told you these things, so that in Me you may have [perfect] peace. In the world you have tribulation and distress and suffering, but be courageous [be confident, be undaunted, be filled with joy]; I have overcome the world." [My conquest is accomplished, My victory abiding.]"
John 16: 33. AMP

We Are Not Exempted from Trouble

"When you pass through the waters, I will be with you; and through the rivers, they will not overwhelm you. When you walk through fire, you will not be scorched, nor will the flame burn you". Isaiah 43: 2. AMP

"There are certain Jews whom you have appointed over the administration of the province of Babylon, namely Shadrach, Meshach, and Abed-ego. These men, O king, pay no attention to you; they do not serve your gods or worship the golden image which you have set up." Then Nebuchadnezzar in a furious rage gave a command to bring Shadrach, Meshach, and Abed-nego; and these men were brought before the king. Nebuchadnezzar said to them, "Is it true, Shadrach, Meshach, and Abed-nego, that you do not serve my gods or worship the golden image which I have set up? Now if you are ready, when you hear the sound of the horn, pipe, lyre, trigon, harp, dulcimer, and all kinds of music, to fall down and worship the image which I have made, very good. But if you do not worship, you shall be thrown at once into the midst of a furnace of blazing fire; and what god is there who can rescue you out of my hands?"

Shadrach, Meshach, and Abed-nego answered the king, "O Nebuchadnezzar, we do not need to answer you on this point. If it be so, our God whom we serve is able to rescue us from the furnace of blazing fire, and He will rescue us from your hand, O king. But even if He does not, let it be known to you, O king, that we are not going to serve your gods or worship the golden image that you have set up!" Then Nebuchadnezzar was filled with fury, and his facial expression changed toward Shadrach, Meshach, and Abed-nego. Then he gave a command that the furnace was to be heated seven times hotter than usual. He commanded certain strong men in his army to tie up Shadrach, Meshach, and Abed-nego and to throw them into the furnace of blazing fire. Then these [three] men were tied up in their trousers, their coats, their turbans, and their other clothes, and were thrown into the midst of the furnace of blazing fire. Because the king's command was urgent and the furnace was extremely hot, the flame of the fire killed the men who carried up Shadrach, Meshach, and Abed-nego. But these three men, Shadrach, Meshach, and Abed-nego, fell into the midst of the furnace of blazing fire still tied up.

Then Nebuchadnezzar the king [looked and] was astounded, and he jumped up and said to his counselors, "Did we not throw three men who were tied up into the midst of the fire?" They replied to the king, "Certainly, O king." He answered, "Look! I see four men untied, walking around in the midst of the fire, and they are not hurt! And the appearance of the fourth is like a son of the gods!" Then Nebuchadnezzar approached the door of the blazing furnace and said, "Shadrach, Meshach, and Abed-nego, servants of the Most-High God, come out [of there]! Come here!" Then Shadrach, Meshach, and Abed-nego came out of the midst of the fire. The satraps, the prefects, the governors, and the king's counselors gathered around them and saw that in regard to these men the fire had no effect on their bodies—their hair was not singed, their clothes were not scorched or damaged, even the smell of smoke was not on them. Nebuchadnezzar responded and said, "Blessed be the God of Shadrach, Meshach, and Abed-nego, who has sent His angel and rescued His servants who believed in, trusted in, and relied on Him! They violated the king's command and surrendered their bodies rather than serve or worship any god except their own God". Daniel 3: 12-28. AMP

Yes, you will pass through the fire (trouble), but God will be there with you. If you will walk through the valley of the shadow of death at one point or another, fear not, because God will be right there with you. God did not stop Shadrach, Meshach, and Abed-nego from going through the fire, but He was right there with them. In fact, Shadrach, Meshach, and Abed-nego came out of the fire, but God did not, He is still there waiting, so that if you ever fall into the fire any time, he will be your present help in time of trouble. Please don't forget that God is the consuming fire Himself. I prayer that God, the consuming fire, consumes any kind of fire the devil throws at you, or plans to throw you into, with His fire and makes you a testimony just like Shadrach, Meshach, and Abed-nego, in Jesus name.

Chapter 6

The Power of Joy

The power of joy is the power of life. The difference is very clear when you see someone whose life is filled with joy and someone filled with the opposite of joy. If you don't know the power of joy, the devil knows by your actions and desires, that is why he will try all the available means possible to steal, kill, or destroy (smash or shatter) your joy. If you are joyful, the presence of light will be evident. When you have the light of joy burning in you, your uplifting gesture, and the elegant smile of your cheerful lips will put on display the glory and the power of joy. Joy has a sweet aroma that emits favor for those that embrace her power and goodness.

Joy Strengthens

Joy strengthens, joy empowers, and joy destroys the yoke of depression, sorrow, shame, and the sting of trouble. The Christian life is not an easy one, it involves walking through valleys and mountain top experiences of life. We are constantly at war with the powers of darkness and yet must love the humans used by the devil to war against us, because our battle is not against flesh and blood. We are not going to win life's battles all the time, there will be times when God will allow us to take life's examination, so He can promote us to our next level of faith, grace, joy, and glory. It is sad to note, how Christians nowadays tend to focus on their sins, its quilt and consequences after sincere repentance; instead of Christ's provision of love, forgiveness, and grace.

It ought to be impossible for a true Christian to accept the state of hopelessness and helplessness, for we can do all things through Jesus Christ who strengthens us. Wow, what a powerful combination, Jesus strengthens us to do all things, and joy strengthens us to enjoy the things God has given us. The best way God likes to silence our enemies of joy is to clothe them with shame, by preparing a table for us before their own eyes while they helplessly watch us enjoy His goodness, grace, and love.

"Then Ezra said to them, "Go [your way], eat the rich festival food, drink the sweet drink, and send portions to him for whom nothing is prepared; for this day is holy to our Lord. And do not be worried, for the joy of the Lord is your strength and your stronghold. The Lord is my Shepherd [to feed, to guide and to shield me], I shall not want. He lets me lie down in green pastures; He leads me beside the still and quiet waters. He refreshes and restores my soul (life); He leads me in the paths of righteousness for His name's sake. Even though I walk through the [sunless] valley of the shadow of death, I fear no evil, for You are with me; Your rod [to protect] and Your staff [to guide], they comfort and console me. You prepare a table before me in the presence of my enemies. You have anointed and refreshed my head with oil; My cup overflows. Surely goodness and mercy and unfailing love shall follow me all the days of my life, and I shall dwell forever [throughout all my days] in the house and in the presence of the Lord".
Nehemiah 8:10; Psalm 23 AMP

Joy Sustains Us

Sustenance, perseverance, and consistency are virtues of success in the Christian race. We all can use divine sustenance any time and any day. The Holy Spirit through God's grace sustains us, comfort us, and helps us to stay focused in the Christian race when we yield ourselves to Him. Thus, we will always stand tall and keep our shoulders high and strong because God is our source of courage and strength when we walk through the valleys of life or death, to combat the enemies of our joy.

"Though the fig tree does not blossom, and there is no fruit on the vines, though the yield of the olive fails, and the fields produce no food, Though the flock is cut off from the fold, and there are no cattle in the stalls, Yet I will [choose to] rejoice in

the Lord; I will [choose to] shout in exultation in the [victorious] God of my salvation! The Lord God is my strength [my source of courage, my invincible army]; He has made my feet [steady and sure] like hinds' feet, and makes me walk [forward with spiritual confidence] on my high places [of challenge and responsibility]. For the choir director, on my stringed instruments." Habakkuk 3:17-19. AMP

Joy Encourages and Motivates

It does not matter how many times you fall, if you can get back up, you are not a loser. You only become a failure if you are not able to rise again. If you have joy, you will be encouraged to press on against all odds, you will be motivated to do more so your joy can be fuller. Every day is a new day filled with hope, blessing, and God's favor. The power of joy improves our lives, and helps us grow in God's grace. We can praise God better when our hearts are filled with joy.

The godly may trip seven times, but they will get up again. But one disaster is enough to overthrow the wicked. This is the day the Lord has made. We will rejoice and be glad in it. Proverbs 24: 16; Psalm 118: 24. NLT

With Joy, We Draw Water from the Springs of Salvation

"Behold, God, my salvation! I will trust and not be afraid, for the Lord God is my strength and song; Yes, He has become my salvation." Therefore, with joy you will draw water from the springs of salvation. May the God of hope fill you with all joy and peace in believing [through the experience of your faith] that by the power of the Holy Spirit you will abound in hope and overflow with confidence in His promises.". Isaiah 12: 2-3; Romans 15: 13. AMP

Joy Refreshes Us after the Night Battles

It does not matter what your enemies plan, how many they are that come against you, they will all fail because God is for you and no weapon formed against you will prosper. The powers of darkness do their planning and outline their strategies at night. Sometimes their plans are executed at night mainly against mature Christians, and others at varying times. All people mostly see are the physical manifestations of the powers of darkness in the day time, they are mainly rolling out what has been concluded during the night. Night gave birth to day, for out of darkness God called out the light. That is why the devil chose night over day light to perfect his evil works. Which explains why a lot of evil takes place at night and why evil agents love to conduct their meetings at night.

A lot of things happen at night because the powers of darkness cannot do much under any kind of lighting. They love to strike at the dead of the night when their dark powers are highly effective because the souls of men are at rest. This is the reason why you must not take your dream life or the nightmares you get sometimes lightly. If you are dealing with *insomnia* only at night something is wrong somewhere, you may be under attack. If you are sleeping long hours and still wake up weak and sickly, something is wrong. God created night for rest, not for our destruction or limitation. You must rise and pray your way through, by destroying the plans and terminating the assignment of the forces of darkness against you. You must take charge of your nights, because the God of the day is also the God of the night. The God of the valley is also the God of the mountains.

Our God rules, be it day or night, He is God Almighty, strong and mighty in battle. Jesus Christ was arrested at night, many believers have fallen from the faith, because of their night experiences powered by the powers of darkness. You must not worry because no matter how hard the enemy tries to weigh you down, God will fight for you, and victory will be yours when the day breaks. You will be refreshed and empowered by the joy of the Lord, for God's mercies are new every morning because He knows you may have exhausted your joy fighting the powers of darkness during the night battles. Many people sleep one night and do not wake up the next morning, because something happened to them during the battles of the night. That will not be your portion in Jesus name. You shall live, you shall not die. God will not only fight for you, His joy will refresh you each morning and empower you to overcome and escape the physical manifestations of the powers of darkness during the day, in Jesus name. If the joy of the Lord is our strength, what happens when we lack joy is the question I have for you. It is safe to say then, if you lack joy, you will lack the power to face your day victoriously. So, embrace joy, be refreshed, and be empowered, so you can be a victor not a loser.

*"For His anger is but for a moment, His favor is for a lifetime. Weeping may endure for a night, but a **shout of joy comes in the morning**. My soul has been cast far away from peace; I have forgotten happiness. So, I say, "My strength has perished and so has my hope and expectation from the Lord." Remember [O Lord] my affliction and my wandering, the wormwood and the gall (bitterness). My soul continually remembers them and is bowed down within me. But this I call to mind; therefore, I have hope. It is because of **the Lord's loving-kindnesses that we are not consumed, because His [tender] compassions never fail. They are new every morning**; Great and beyond measure is Your faithfulness. "The Lord is my portion and my inheritance," says my soul; "Therefore I have hope in Him and wait expectantly for Him"".* Psalm 30:5; Lamentation 3: 17-24. AMP

Chapter 7

Some Things That Can Limit Your Joy

The devil is working ceaselessly with everything he's got to limit, steal, kill, or destroy your joy. There are a lot of ammunitions at the devil's disposal that he can use at any given time to limit your joy if you let him. Though Jesus Christ overcame him (the devil) through His death and resurrection, you must not underestimate the determination of the devil to use his best tricks, deception, and any available human artillery (agents) to fight against you at any time. Sometimes all we see around us is despair, fear and uncertainty, which the devil wants us to embrace, they are in fact traps, obstacles or roadblocks to our joy if we make room for them in our lives. The enemies of joy will stop at nothing until they see you miserable, discouraged, and unfruitful in your Christian race.

Jealousy and Envy

We live in a world where material wealth, professional success, and social accomplishments serve as the standards for happiness and joy. Some of us are being manipulated by the devil into becoming jealous of other people's achievements. Jealousy consumes joy and happiness, and often leads to the path of destruction. Relationships targeted with the arrows of jealousy and envy often end with pain and sorrow. Covetousness and jealousy are demonic partners with envy; on a mission to truncate our success, happiness, and joy. Jealous, and envious people are sad and angry when others are happy or joyful. God hates jealousy and envy. People who are jealous and envious are those whose joy has been truncated, and they want others to be like them. The bible says those who practice jealous and envy are yet to transformed by the Holy Spirit, in other words they are operating in the flesh and still worldly.

"You are still worldly [controlled by ordinary impulses, the sinful capacity]. For as long as there is jealousy and

strife and discord among you, are you not unspiritual, and are you not walking like ordinary men [unchanged by faith]?" 1 Corinthians 3:3. AMP

Pleasing People over God

Christians who enjoy pleasing people over God are everywhere. Starting from the pulpit to the pew, all the way down to the ungodly. People who please people over God do so, to be loved, recognized, and accepted by humans not by God. They are caught in the web of satanic deception that if they fail to please people, they will be rejected, unappreciated and unloved. They allow the feelings and the happiness of others to determine their own action, reaction, and false lifestyle fabrication. They long with passion for human approval to gratify their emotional greed, lust and pride directly or indirectly.

The truth is that people pleasers are unhappy, the absence of joy in their lives leads them to the self-delusion that their joy and happiness springs from what others think about them or what others perceive of them and view or see in them. It is unhealthy and ungodly to live one's life or value solely on the acceptance, approval, or the affirmation of others. It is deception to believe that your joy comes from fellow humans like you. God takes the glory, honor and praise due Him very seriously, and if you are giving what belongs to Him to mankind, you may be in grave danger of getting into trouble with God.

"Am I now trying to win the favor and approval of men, or of God? Or am I seeking to please someone? If I were still trying to be popular with men, I would not be a bond-servant of Christ." Galatians 1: 10. AMP

Worries

Worry is often the byproduct of anxiety, fear, and intimidation, fueled by frustration, disappointment and discouragement; yes, and of course satanic attacks. God never promised us a life void of distress, pressure, and trouble. He did promise He will be with us when we go through the fire of adversity, hardship or the valley of the shadow of death. Worry is a very wide subject and time will fail us to dig deep into the symptoms of its destructive ways. Worries can kill not only your joy, but your soul, and so does fear.

"'Do not fear [anything], for I am with you; Do not be afraid, for I am your God. I will strengthen you, be assured I will help you; I will certainly take hold of you with My righteous right hand [hand of justice, of power, of victory, of salvation].' And not only this, but [with joy] let us exult in our sufferings and rejoice in our hardships, knowing that hardship (distress, pressure, trouble) produces patient endurance; and endurance, proven character (spiritual maturity); and proven character, hope and confident assurance [of eternal salvation]. Such hope [in God's promises] never disappoints us, because God's love has been abundantly poured out within our hearts through the Holy Spirit who was given to us."
Isaiah 41:10; Romans 5: 3-5. AMP

"Do not be anxious or worried about anything, but in everything [every circumstance and situation] by prayer and petition with thanksgiving, continue to make your [specific] requests known to God. And the peace of God [that peace which reassures the heart, that peace] which transcends all understanding, [that peace which] stands guard over your hearts and your minds in Christ Jesus [is yours].

Finally, believers, whatever is true, whatever is honorable and worthy of respect, whatever is right and confirmed by God's word, whatever is pure and wholesome, whatever is lovely and brings peace, whatever is admirable and of good repute; if there is any excellence, if there is anything worthy of praise, think continually on these things [center your mind on them, and implant them in your heart]." Philippians 4:6-8. AMP

Doubt and Unbelief

Doubt and unbelief are a double-edged sword used by the devil to keep humanity in the bondage of fear, worries, and discouragement. Doubt and unbelief affirms that worldly or human alternatives are better and easier than God's ways or directives in His word. The sin of doubt and unbelief is Satan's greatest ammunition against all children of God. That evil snake turned dragon brought down the first Adam with doubt and unbelief, and none of us in this world can overcome its deadly venom without the help of Jesus Christ. Every time we doubt God or succumb to unbelief we begin to sink just like Peter did in the bible.

"When the disciples saw Him walking on the sea, they were terrified, and said, "It is a ghost!" And they cried out in fear. But immediately He spoke to them, saying, "Take courage, it is I! Do not be afraid!" Peter replied to Him, "Lord, if it is [really] You, command me to come to You on the water." He said, "Come!" So, Peter got out of the boat, and walked on the water and came toward Jesus. But when he saw [the effects of] the wind, he was frightened, and he began to sink, and he cried out, "Lord, save me!" Immediately Jesus extended His hand and caught him, saying to him, "O you of little faith, why did you doubt?" And when they got into the boat, the wind ceased. Then those in the boat worshiped Him [with awe-inspired reverence], saying, "Truly You are the Son of God!"

Now early in the morning, as Jesus was coming back to the city, He was hungry. Seeing a lone fig tree at the roadside, He went to it and found nothing but leaves on it; and He said to it, "Never again will fruit come from you." And at once the fig tree withered. When the disciples saw it, they were astonished and asked, "How is it that the fig tree has withered away all at once?" Jesus replied to them, "I assure you and most solemnly say to you, if you have faith [personal trust and confidence in Me] and do not doubt or allow yourself to be drawn in two directions, you will not only do what was done to the fig tree, but even if you say to this mountain, 'Be taken up and thrown into the sea,' it will happen [if God wills it]...But he must ask [for wisdom] in faith, without doubting [God's willingness to help], for the one who doubts is like a billowing surge of the sea that is blown about and tossed by the wind.

For such a person ought not to think or expect that he will receive anything [at all] from the Lord, being a double-minded man, unstable and restless in all his ways [in everything he thinks, feels, or decides]." Matthew 14:26-33; 21: 18-21; James 1:6-8. AMP

Evil Association

Evil association often leads to pretense (self-deception), sowing seeds of discords, and negative influence. Evil association is just as bad as evil communication, both are conceived in the womb of deception, lust, and greed. My father once told me a long time ago, that evil association corrupts good manners. I found out later that the quotation was actually taken from 1 Corinthians 15 verse 33 *"Do not be deceived: "Bad company corrupts good morals"*. The same is true of evil communication. To avoid evil communication and association is the sole reason why God does not want His children to be on equal yokes (the same level) with unbelievers; simply because it is impossible for light and darkness to be the same. Don't allow evil association or communication to corrupt or spoil your joy.

"Be steadfast and very determined to keep and to do everything that is written in the Book of the Law of Moses, so that you do not turn aside from it to the right or the left, so that you do not associate with these nations which remain among you, or mention the name of their gods, or make anyone swear [an oath by them], or serve them, or bow down to them. But you are to cling to the Lord your God, just as you have done to this day. For the Lord has driven out great and mighty nations from before you; and as for you, no man has been able to stand [in opposition] before you to this day. One of your men puts to

44

flight a thousand, for the Lord your God is He who is fighting for you, just as He promised you. So be very careful and watchful of yourselves to love the Lord your God. For if you ever turn back and cling to the rest of these nations, these that are left among you, and intermarry with them, so that you associate with them and they with you, know and understand with certainty that the Lord your God will not continue to drive these nations out from before you; but they will be a snare and trap to you, and a whip on your sides and thorns in your eyes, until you perish from this good land which the Lord your God has given you.

"Now behold, today I am going the way of all the earth, and you know in all your hearts and in all your souls that not one word of all the good words which the Lord your God has promised concerning you has failed; all have been fulfilled for you, not one of them has failed. It shall come about that just as every good word which the Lord your God spoke and promised to you has been fulfilled for you, so the Lord will bring upon you every bad thing [about which He warned you], until He has destroyed and eliminated you from this good land which the Lord your God has given you. When you transgress (violate) the covenant of the Lord your God, which He commanded you [to follow], and you go and serve other gods and bow down to them, then the anger of the Lord will be kindled against you, and you shall perish quickly from the good land which He has given you." Joshua 23:6-16. AMP

Not Abiding in Christ

Failing to abide in Christ as a Christian could cause you more pain than a headache would. If you and I are not abiding in Christ, we are not yet His disciples. It simply means we are not yet broken, still trying to live in the world and be in Christ at the same time. Your joy will never be full unless you abide in Christ. If you are willing to settle for a handful drops of joy instead of a river full of joy, that is totally up to you.

"I am the true Vine, and My Father is the vine-dresser. Every branch in Me that does not bear fruit, He takes away; and every branch that continues to bear fruit, He [repeatedly]
prunes, so that it will bear more fruit [even richer and finer fruit]. You are already clean because of the word which I have given you [the teachings which I have discussed with you]. Remain in Me, and I [will remain] in you. Just as no branch can bear fruit by itself without remaining in the vine, neither can you [bear fruit, producing evidence of your faith] unless you remain in Me. I am the Vine; you are the branches. The one who remains in Me and I in him bears much fruit, for [otherwise] apart from Me [that is, cut off from vital union with Me] you can do nothing. If anyone does not remain in Me, he is thrown out like a [broken off] branch, and withers and dies; and they gather such branches and throw them into the fire, and they are burned.

If you remain in Me and My words remain in you [that is, if we are vitally united and My message lives in your heart], ask whatever you wish and it will be done for you. My Father is glorified and honored by this, when you bear much fruit, and prove yourselves to be My [true] disciples. I have loved you just as the Father has loved Me; remain in My love [and do not doubt My love for you]. If you keep My commandments
and obey My teaching, you will remain in My love, just as I have kept My Father's commandments and remain in His love. I have told you these things so that My joy and delight may be in you, and that your joy may be made full and complete and overflowing". John 15:1-11. AMP

46

Chapter 8

Defending Your Joy

The best way you and I can defend our joy, is to abide in Christ. To defend our joy, we must put on the whole armor of God if we must overcome the devil and his agents fighting day and night to steal, kill, or destroy our joy with his nuclear-powered tricks. We will always subdue Satan any time, if we are in good standing with God.

"For though we walk in the flesh [as mortal men], we are not carrying on our [spiritual] warfare according to the flesh and using the weapons of man. The weapons of our warfare are not physical [weapons of flesh and blood]. Our weapons are divinely powerful for the destruction of fortresses. We are destroying sophisticated arguments and every exalted and proud thing that sets itself up against the [true] knowledge of God, and we are taking every thought and purpose captive to the obedience of Christ, being ready to punish every act of disobedience, when your own obedience [as a church] is complete". 2 Corinthians 10:3-6. AMP

Put on the Whole Armor of God

"In conclusion, be strong in the Lord [draw your strength from Him and be empowered through your union with Him] and in the power of His [boundless] might. Put on the full armor of God [for His precepts are like the splendid armor of a heavily-armed soldier], so that you may be able to [successfully] stand up against all the schemes and the strategies and the deceits of the devil. For our struggle is not against flesh and blood [contending only with physical opponents], but against the rulers, against the powers, against the world forces of this [present] darkness, against the spiritual forces of wickedness in the heavenly (supernatural) places.

Therefore, put on the complete armor of God, so that you will be able to [successfully] resist and stand your ground in the evil day [of danger], and having done everything [that the crisis demands], to stand firm [in your place, fully prepared, immovable, victorious]. So, stand firm and hold your ground, having tightened the wide band of truth (personal integrity, moral courage) around your waist and having put on the breastplate of righteousness (an upright heart), and having strapped on your feet the gospel of peace in preparation [to face the enemy with firm-footed stability and the readiness produced by the good news].

Above all, lift up the [protective] shield of faith with which you can extinguish all the flaming arrows of the evil one. And take the helmet of salvation, and the sword of the Spirit, which is the Word of God. With all prayer and petition pray [with specific requests] at all times [on every occasion and in every season] in the Spirit, and with this in view, stay alert with all perseverance and petition [interceding in prayer] for all God's people". Ephesian 6: 10-18. AMP

Apostle Paul Fought the Enemies of His Joy and Prevailed

Five times I received from [the hands of] the Jews forty [lashes all] but one; Three times I have been beaten with rods; once I was stoned. Three times I have been aboard a ship wrecked at sea; a [whole] night and a day I have spent [adrift] on the deep; Many times on journeys, [exposed to] perils from rivers, perils from bandits, perils from [my own] nation, perils from the Gentiles, perils in the city, perils in the desert places, perils in the sea, perils from those posing as believers [but destitute of Christian knowledge and piety]; In toil and hardship, watching often [through sleepless nights], in hunger and thirst, frequently driven to fasting by want, in cold and exposure and lack of clothing.

For God Who said, let light shine out of darkness, has shone in our hearts so as [to beam forth] the Light for the illumination of the knowledge of the majesty and glory of God [as it is manifested in the Person and is revealed] in the face of Jesus Christ (the Messiah). However, we possess this precious treasure [the divine Light of the Gospel] in [frail, human] vessels of earth, that the grandeur and exceeding greatness of the power may be shown to be from God and not from ourselves. We are hedged in (pressed) on every side [troubled and oppressed in every way], but not cramped or crushed; we suffer embarrassments and are perplexed and unable to find a way out, but not driven to despair; We are pursued (persecuted and hard driven), but not deserted [to stand alone]; we are struck down to the ground, but never struck out and destroyed.

Always carrying about in the body the liability and exposure to the same putting to death that the Lord Jesus suffered, so that the [resurrection] life of Jesus also may be shown forth by and in our bodies. For we who live are constantly [experiencing] being handed over to death for Jesus' sake, that the [resurrection] life of Jesus also may be evidenced through our flesh which is liable to death. Thus, death is actively at work in us, but [it is in order that our] life [may be actively at work] in you. Yet we have the same spirit of faith as he had who wrote, I have believed, and therefore have I spoken. We too believe, and therefore we speak". 2 Corinthians 11:24-27; 4: 6-13. AMPC

Soldier of Christ, Fight for Your Joy

The apostle Paul also makes it clear that the Christian's commitment to Jesus Christ our Commander in chief ought to be more, real and complete more than that of any earthly soldier.

"Take with me your share of hardship [passing through the difficulties which you are called to endure], like a good soldier of Christ Jesus. No soldier in active service gets entangled in the [ordinary business] affairs of civilian life; [he avoids them] so that he may please the one who enlisted him to serve".

2 Timothy 2:3-4. AMP

Fight the Good Fight of Faith

Not all the fights we fight nowadays are good fights. Any fight we fight because of, or out of lust, pride and greed are not the good fight of faith. The good fight is working out your salvation with fear and trembling, defending your faith, love for the Lord, and joy. Remember we do not run the Christian race by the world's standards, but by God's standards, in spirit and in truth.

"Do you not know that in a race all the runners run [their very best to win], but only one receives the prize? Run [your race] in such a way that you may seize the prize and make it yours! Now every athlete who [goes into training and] competes in the games is disciplined and exercises self-control in all things. They do it to win a crown that withers, but we [do it to receive] an imperishable [crown that cannot wither]. Therefore, I do not run without a definite goal; I do not flail around like one beating the air [just shadow boxing]. But [like a boxer] I strictly discipline my body and make it my slave, so that, after I have preached [the gospel] to others, I myself will not somehow be disqualified [as unfit for service]. Fight the good fight of the faith [in the conflict with evil]; take hold of the eternal life to which you were called, and [for which] you made the good confession [of faith] in the presence of many witnesses. I solemnly charge you in the presence of God, who gives life to all things, and [in the presence] of Christ Jesus, who made the good confession [in His testimony] before Pontius Pilate, to keep all His precepts without stain or reproach until the appearing of our Lord Jesus Christ". 1 Corinthians 9:24-27; 1 Timothy 6:12-14 AMP

Fight Like David to Secure the Joy of Your family

"As he was talking with them, behold, the champion, the Philistine of Gath named Goliath, was coming up from the army of the Philistines, and he spoke these same words again; and

David heard him. When the men of Israel all saw the man, they fled from him, and were very frightened. The men of Israel said, "Have you seen this man who is coming up? Surely, he is coming up to defy Israel. The king will reward the man who kills him with great riches, and will give him his daughter [in marriage] and make his father's house (family) free [from taxes and service] in Israel." Then David spoke to the men who were standing by him, "What will be done for the man who kills this Philistine and removes the disgrace [of his taunting] from Israel? For who is this uncircumcised Philistine that he has taunted and defied the armies of the living God?" Then he took his [shepherd's] staff in his hand and chose for himself five smooth stones out of the stream bed, and put them in his shepherd's bag which he had, that is, in his shepherd's pouch. With his sling in his hand, he approached the Philistine.

The Philistine came and approached David, with his shield-bearer in front of him. When the Philistine looked around and saw David, he derided and disparaged him because he was [just] a young man, with a ruddy complexion, and a handsome appearance. The Philistine said to David, "Am I a dog, that you come to me with [shepherd's] staffs?" And the Philistine cursed David by his gods. The Philistine also said to David, "Come to me, and I will give your flesh to the birds of the sky and the beasts of the field." Then David said to the Philistine, "You come to me with a sword, a spear, and a javelin, but I come to you in the name of the Lord of hosts, the God of the armies of Israel, whom you have taunted. This day the Lord will hand you over to me, and I will strike you down and cut off your head. And I will give the corpses of the army of the Philistines this day to the birds of the sky and the wild beasts of the earth, so that all the earth may know that there is a God in Israel, and that this entire assembly may know that the Lord does not save with the sword or with the spear; for the battle is the Lord's and He will hand you over to us."

52

When the Philistine rose, and came forward to meet David, David ran quickly toward the battle line to meet the Philistine. David put his hand into his bag and took out a stone and slung it, and it struck the Philistine on his forehead. The stone penetrated his forehead, and he fell face down on the ground. So, David triumphed over the Philistine with a sling and a stone, and he struck down the Philistine and killed him; but there was no sword in David's hand. So, he ran and stood over the Philistine, grasped his sword and drew it out of its sheath and killed him, and cut off his head with it. When the Philistines saw that their [mighty] champion was dead, they fled".
1 Samuel 17:23-26; 1 Samuel 17: 40-51. AMP

Live in and by God's Word

The word of God is alive and powerful. Jesus is the Word of God. God's word is your spiritual sword which you can use to slay every Goliath fighting against your joy and peace. During Jesus' physical earthly days, the sword was the most common weapon used for battle. God's word (sword of the Spirit) is a two-edged sword; which can be used as a defensive and as an offensive weapon in all spiritual and physical life battles.

"For the word of God is living and active and full of power [making it operative, energizing, and effective]. It is sharper than any two-edged sword, penetrating as far as the division of the soul and spirit [the completeness of a person], and of both joints and marrow [the deepest parts of our nature], exposing and judging the very thoughts and intentions of the heart".
Hebrews 4:12. AMP

Jesus' Word is Absolute and Ultimate Power

In fact, when Jesus comes back for the final destruction of the powers of darkness, He will use His Word to conquer. Jesus first came as the Lamb of God, now He will be coming as the Loin of Judah.

"And I saw heaven opened, and behold, a white horse, and He who was riding it is called Faithful and True (trustworthy, loyal, incorruptible, steady), and in righteousness He judges

and wages war [on the rebellious nations]. His eyes are a flame of fire, and on His head are many royal crowns; and He has a name inscribed [on Him] which no one knows or understands except Himself. He is dressed in a robe dipped in blood, and His name is called The Word of God. And the armies of heaven, dressed in fine linen, [dazzling] white and clean, followed Him on white horses. From His mouth comes a sharp sword (His word) with which He may strike down the nations, and He will rule them with a rod of iron; and He will tread the wine press of the fierce wrath of God, the Almighty [in judgment of the rebellious world]. And on His robe and on His thigh He has a name inscribed, "KING OF KINGS, AND LORD OF LORDS."

Then I saw a single angel standing in the sun, and with a loud voice he shouted to all the birds that fly in midheaven, saying, "Come, gather together for the great supper of God, so that you may feast on the flesh of kings, the flesh of commanders, the flesh of powerful and mighty men, the flesh of horses and of those who sit on them, and the flesh of all humanity, both free men and slaves, both small and great [in a complete conquest of evil]." Then I saw the beast and the kings and political leaders of the earth with their armies gathered to make war against Him who is mounted on the [white] horse and against His army. And the beast (Antichrist) was seized and overpowered, and with him the false prophet who, in his presence, had performed [amazing] signs by which he deceived those who had received the mark of the beast and those who worshiped his image; these two were hurled alive into the lake of fire which blazes with brimstone. And the rest were killed with the sword which came from the mouth of Him who sat on the horse, and all the birds fed ravenously and gorged themselves with their flesh". Revelation 19:11-21. AMP

Always Watch and Pray

No matter how powerful you think you are, don't fail to watch and pray. For even the best of armor becomes useless if the Christian soldier falls asleep in the battlefield of life. When we lack prayer, we lack power. Failing to pray is planning to fail. Those who don't pray often become prey for the roaring lions of lust, pride, greed, and deception.

"Be on guard and stay constantly alert [and pray]; for you do not know when the appointed time will come. Keep actively watching and praying that you may not come into temptation; the spirit is willing, but the body is weak." Be sober [well balanced and self-disciplined], be alert and cautious at all times. That enemy of yours, the devil, prowls around like a roaring lion [fiercely hungry], seeking someone to devour. But resist him, be firm in your faith [against his attack—rooted, established, immovable], knowing that the same experiences of suffering are being experienced by your brothers and sisters throughout the world. [You do not suffer alone.]"
Mark 13:33; Matthew 26:41; 1 Peter 5:8-9. AMP

Chapter 9

Some Ways You Can Improve Your Joy

The good Lord has provided you and I many ways and means to improve our joy. One thing that is very crucial here is that you can only improve on what you already have and in your control. What you've lost is outside of your control, you cannot improve upon it. King David once lost his joy at a time when he was going through his own life's challenges and difficulties. In King David's case, he had committed adultery, and attempted to cover up his sin, and he committed murder in the process. God did not take this issue lightly with King David, the anger of God was poured out against David and Israel. David's soul was terribly crushed, deeply troubled, and he lost his joy. King David cried out to God and pleaded wholeheartedly for mercy and for his joy to be restored back to him.

"Give me back [Restore to me] the joy of your salvation [rescue]. Keep me strong by giving [Sustain in] me a willing spirit". Psalm 51: 12. EXB

Here Are Some Ways You Can Improve Your Joy

We are all humans, yet we are all unique beings. What works very well for me may not produce the same result for you or may produce greater results for you, because the levels of our faith, and strength of belief may not be the same. The ways that are listed and explained in this book to improve your joy are all scripturally based, and time tested. If you prayerfully apply them, they have been proven to work if applied with integrity, faith, and determination with the help of the Holy Spirit.

1. Be thankful and grateful

Thanksgiving is the expression of gratitude, in appreciation of God's goodness, love, and kindness toward us. It is good to give thanks to God for the many blessings of salvation. Giving thanks gives us the opportunity to demonstrate our faith in God, and our love for Him. We should learn to be thankful for one another too, because expressing gratitude to others will help appreciate God's grace in them. Those who don't give thanks are those who don't take time to think. You are powerless in yourself if not for the life God has given you. Tell me how much a man in a coma in the hospital can accomplish in sport, business, or wealth accumulation? We should always be grateful, for it is the secret antibiotics to cure the sickness of the opposites of joy and promote your physical good health. We can also express our thanks to God through praise and worship. It is impossible to be merry and sad the same time, for a merry heart can do wonders and great good like medicine to the soul.

"A merry heart does good, like medicine, but a broken spirit dries the bones. Make a joyful shout to the Lord, all you lands! Serve the Lord with gladness; Come before His presence with singing. Know that the Lord, He is God; It is He who has made us, and not we ourselves; We are His people and the sheep of His pasture. Enter into His gates with thanksgiving, and into His courts with praise. Be thankful to Him, and bless His name. For the Lord is good; His mercy is everlasting, and His truth endures to all generations. Bless the Lord, O my soul; and all that is within me, bless His holy name! Bless the Lord, O my soul, and forget not all His benefits: Who forgives all your iniquities, who heals all your diseases, who redeems your life from destruction, who crowns you with lovingkindness and tender mercies, who satisfies your mouth with good things, so that your youth is renewed like the eagle's.

The Lord executes righteousness and justice for all who are oppressed. He made known His ways to Moses, His acts to the children of Israel. The Lord is merciful and gracious, slow to anger, and abounding in mercy. He will not always strive with us, nor will He keep His anger forever. He has not dealt with us according to our sins, nor punished us according to our iniquities. For as the heavens are high above the earth, so great is His mercy toward those who fear Him; As far as the east is from the west, so far has He removed our transgressions from us.

As a father pities his children, so the Lord pities those who fear Him. For He knows our frame; He remembers that we are dust. As for man, his days are like grass; As a flower of the field, so he flourishes. For the wind passes over it, and it is gone, and its place remembers it no more. but the mercy of the Lord is from everlasting to everlasting on those who fear Him, and His righteousness to children's children, to such as keep His covenant, and to those who remember His commandments to do them. The Lord has established His throne in heaven, and His kingdom rules over all. Bless the Lord, you His angels, who excel in strength, who do His word, heeding the voice of His word. Bless the Lord, all you His hosts, you ministers of His, who do His pleasure. Bless the Lord, all His works, in all places of His dominion. Bless the Lord, O my soul!" Proverbs 17:22; Psalm 100; 103. NKJV

2. Embrace a Positive Attitude

You and I may agree that dealing with difficult people is not always easy, and that a negative attitude never brings joy to any relationship. In fact, having a negative attitude keeps us from being happy, truncates our joy, and makes us a suspect as an enemy of joy. On the other hand, we understand that positive attitude has a direct connection to happiness, joy, and success. I think it is safe to say that your way of life and how well others relate to you reflects in your attitude. Negative attitude can prevent you from enjoying your life, God's goodness, blessings and joy, because God often works through people. If you really want to make the company of people around you lovely, respectful, and accommodating, you should examine your own attitude toward them. Learn to be good at managing rejection without feeling rejected, but as a learning process to improve upon.

Don't let yourself get dragged into other people's complaints or become influenced by their negativity fellowship, nor join forces with them by becoming negative yourself. In times of tragedy, show love and kindness. It is sad to note that we often come together to do good when natural disasters, war, and traumatic experiences occur. If you can love and show kindness to your family, friends, co-workers and neighbors daily; what a blessing that would bring to your own life. It often looks like we are pretending whenever, pain, fear, and devastation are what brings out the goodness, love, and kindness in us. Don't wait for something bad to happen first before you show love and try to put a smile on people's face, let joy be your reason for showing love and kindness. Don't always be problems minded, be solution minded. Any time you are prompted to point out problems in the lives of others, ask God for grace to help you be on hand to help them find a solution. Pointing out problems without providing possible ways to solve them will create problems for you and for others until the problems are resolved.

Never criticism people to make them look bad, it will make you look bad, and makes you look like a problem starter. Positive people use constructive criticism to improve conditions not to make them worse. If you are going to point out problems in people or situations, please trust God to help you help them find solutions as well. Instead of pointing out the things that are wrong or mistakes, offer ways to help them get better. Make it your goal to make others smile, and you will not lack smiles. When you make others happy, you are creating a happy environment around yourself, and building a wall against the enemies of joy. To embrace a positive attitude, you must also embrace the golden rule that says, "Treat others the same way you would want others to treat you". I took time to stress the above because I was a victim and now I am a helper by God's grace.

"So then, in everything treat others the same way you want them to treat you, for this is [the essence of] the Law and the [writings of the] Prophets. Do not be deceived, God is not mocked [He will not allow Himself to be ridiculed, nor treated with contempt nor allow His precepts to be scornfully set aside]; for whatever a man sows, this and this only is what he will reap. For the one who sows to his flesh [his sinful capacity, his worldliness, his disgraceful impulses] will reap from the flesh ruin and destruction, but the one who sows to the Spirit will from the Spirit reap eternal life. Let us not grow weary or become discouraged in doing good, for at the proper time we will reap, if we do not give in. So then, while we [as individual believers] have the opportunity, let us do good to all people [not only being helpful, but also doing that which promotes their spiritual well-being], and especially [be a blessing] to those of the household of faith (born-again believers)".
Matthew 7:12; Galatians 6:7-10 AMP

3. Put God First in Your Life

A lot of things clamor and contend for our attention and focus daily; family, jobs, friends, and enemies. It is our responsibility to fight against distractions and filter our demands ranging from luxury, wants, and needs. We must be very careful not to allow our earthly demands to impede our relationship with God. If we are not very careful, we can easily be caught in the web of deception. The devil enjoys distracting us from truth into believing in his lies. Sometimes we tend to put ourselves first, when we know without a doubt we only have hopes and dreams because we have life—the life that God has given us. Selfishness, lust, greed, and pride are the end time armies of the devil. Many great and mighty, rich and poor, old and young have been crushed by the above, ranging from their cradle lives to their life's pinnacles. Whenever the devil gets a good opportunity to launch any attack on God's children, he strikes with precision, especially during rest and peace times. Our weapons of war against the enemies of our joy, peace, and life are useless against the devil and his evil agents without God. Our weapons are only strong through God, which is the main reason why we must learn to always put God first in our lives.

Though Jesus came that we may have life and have it more abundantly, really it is you and I who call the shots; because the key to you and I enjoying the abundant life Jesus gives is by giving Him the first place in our lives. God is faithful and will not fail to keep His promises to us. It is completely up to us to seek His kingdom first and then His righteousness, so that all other things—joy inclusive will be given to us. We discovered in chapter one of this book that God is the source of our joy. We will not get God's best and fullness if we don't put God first in our lives. The good news is, it is never too late to put God first, God is always ready with open arms and hands of love and mercy to receive us back and give us a second chance.

"Do not store up for yourselves [material] treasures on earth, where moth and rust destroy, and where thieves break in and steal. But store up for yourselves treasures in heaven, where neither moth nor rust destroys, and where thieves do not break in and steal; for where your treasure is, there your heart [your wishes, your desires; that on which your life centers] will be also. But first and most importantly seek (aim at, strive after) His kingdom and His righteousness [His way of doing and being right—the attitude and character of God], and all these things will be given to you also."
Matthew 6:19-21, 33. AMP

4. Learn to Persevere

Perseverance is the grace given to us by God to persist in anything we undertake; to maintain a purpose and to stand against life's odds, by continuing steadfastly and courageously through the comfort and power of the Holy Spirit. To reduce life's odds against you, you must be lovable and loving to attract love. Be a peacemaker if you want peace to reign in your own life. Take good care of yourself, so you will have the strength, will, and courage to take good care of others. If you are not good to yourself, it may be impossible for you to be trusted to be of any good to others. If you can persevere in these tasks, persevering in other areas of your life will not be too difficult for you to handle as you grow in grace.

"For this very reason, applying your diligence [to the divine promises, make every effort] in [exercising] your faith to, develop moral excellence, and in moral excellence, knowledge (insight, understanding), and in your knowledge, self-control, and in your self-control, steadfastness, and in your steadfastness, godliness, and in your godliness, brotherly affection, and in your brotherly affection, [develop Christian] love [that is, learn to unselfishly seek the best for others and to do things for their benefit]. For as these qualities are yours and are increasing [in you as you grow toward spiritual maturity], they will keep you from being useless and unproductive about the true knowledge and greater understanding of our Lord Jesus Christ. For whoever lacks these qualities is blind—shortsighted [closing his spiritual eyes to the truth], having become oblivious to the fact that he was cleansed from his old sins".
2 Peter 1:5-9. AMP

Chapter 10

How You Can Secure Your Joy

As Christians, we are daily at war, it is called spiritual warfare. You as a soldier of Christ must put on your armor and be always ready in a combat mood to fight and wrestle down any satanic forces that come against your joy, life, and family, in Jesus name. It will be impossible for us to recover and restore the joy and testimonies that the devil and his evil agents have stolen if we don't overcome the devil and his evil agents first by the blood of the Lamb and the words of our testimonies—God's word.

"How can anyone go into a strong man's house and steal his property unless he first overpowers and ties up the strong man? Then he will ransack and rob his house. And they overcame and conquered him because of the blood of the Lamb and because of the word of their testimony, for they did not love their life and renounce their faith even when faced with death". Matthew 12:29; Revelation 12:11. AMP

Soldiers don't go to war without proper planning. As Christians, we must examine our weapons (Christian armor) of war. The reason why many of us lose to the enemies of joy is because we keep fighting in the flesh—*with our carnal minds.* The truth is that we do not fight against one another, but against the devil who uses some of us to act directly or indirectly. The devil is always ready to devour if he is given the opportunity through lust, pride, greed, and evil association.

We Fight Against Spiritual Forces of Darkness

"In conclusion, be strong in the Lord [draw your strength from Him and be empowered through your union with Him] and in the power of His [boundless] might. Put on the full armor of God [for His precepts are like the splendid armor of a heavily-armed soldier], so that you may be able to [successfully] stand

up against all the schemes and the strategies and the deceits of the devil. For our struggle is not against flesh and blood [contending only with physical opponents], but against the rulers, against the powers, against the world forces of this [present] darkness, against the spiritual forces of wickedness in the heavenly (supernatural) places. Therefore, put on the complete armor of God, so that you will be able to [successfully] resist and stand your ground in the evil day [of danger], and having done everything [that the crisis demands], to stand firm [in your place, fully prepared, immovable, victorious].

So, stand firm and hold your ground, having tightened the wide band of truth (personal integrity, moral courage) around your waist and having put on the breastplate of righteousness (an upright heart), and having strapped on your feet the gospel of peace in preparation [to face the enemy with firm-footed stability and the readiness produced by the good news]. Above all, lift up the [protective] shield of faith with which you can extinguish all the flaming arrows of the evil one. And take the helmet of salvation, and the sword of the Spirit, which is the Word of God. With all prayer and petition pray [with specific requests] at all times [on every occasion and in every season] in the Spirit, and with this in view, stay alert with all perseverance and petition [interceding in prayer] for all God's people." Ephesians 6: 10-18. AMP

Lack of Spiritual Warfare Knowledge Is Dangerous

Ignorance has been classified by the experts as a disease that must be cured with knowledge. Any Child of God who thinks Spiritual warfare is child's play does not understand that his or her life, joy, and peace may very well depend on his or her victory in the spirit. Many of us Christians die from accidents, sicknesses, and diseases when our God is the physician (Our healer) and great defender (Our refuge and fortress) because of lack of Knowledge.

*"Therefore, **My people go into exile because they lack knowledge [of God]**; And their honorable men are famished, And their common people are parched with thirst. Therefore Sheol (the realm of the dead) has increased its appetite and opened its mouth beyond measure; And Jerusalem's splendor, her multitude, her [boisterous] uproar and her [drunken] revelers descend into it. So, the common man will be bowed down and the man of importance degraded, and the eyes of the proud (arrogant) will be degraded. **My people are destroyed for lack of knowledge [of My law, where I reveal My will]**. Because you [the priestly nation] have rejected knowledge, I will also reject you from being My priest. Since you have forgotten the law of your God, I will also forget your children. With his mouth the godless man destroys his neighbor, **but through knowledge and discernment the righteous will be rescued"**.*
Isaiah 5:13-15; Hosea 4:6; Proverbs 11:9. AMP

Our Greatest Battle Is Internal
Child of God, our greatest battle is not external but internal, the battle of life rages in you in your heart and mind. So, if you must secure and enjoy your joy, the abundant life God has given you through Christ, you must submit yourself totally to God. The battle of life rages in our minds, feelings, or emotions, and in our flesh. Satan will keep trying to pull you back into sin, so he can get access into your life to steal, kill, and destroy your joy. Oh, how sad it is, that many of us choose to turn to alcohol, drugs, materialism, and sex; instead of turning to God to fight alongside with us till we get the victory. There is no time in history that sin has conquered sin, what is born of the flesh is flesh and that which is born of the spirit is spirit. We cannot fight in the flesh and expect to get victory in the spirit. The weapons of our warfare are not carnal—fleshly functioned, but they are mighty through God in Christ.

"We must not tempt the Lord [that is, test His patience, question His purpose or exploit His goodness], as some of them did—and they were killed by serpents. And do not murmur [in

unwarranted discontent], as some of them did—and were destroyed by the destroyer. Now these things happened to them as an example and warning [to us]; they were written for our instruction [to admonish and equip us], upon whom the ends of the ages have come. Therefore, let the one who thinks he stands firm [immune to temptation, being overconfident and self-righteous], take care that he does not fall [into sin and condemnation].

No temptation [regardless of its source] has overtaken or enticed you that is not common to human experience [nor is any temptation unusual or beyond human resistance]; but God is faithful [to His word—He is compassionate and trustworthy], and He will not let you be tempted beyond your ability [to resist], but along with the temptation He [has in the past and is now and] will [always] provide the way out as well, so that you will be able to endure it [without yielding, and will overcome temptation with joy].

The weapons of our warfare are not physical [weapons of flesh and blood]. Our weapons are divinely powerful for the destruction of fortresses. We are destroying sophisticated arguments and every exalted and proud thing that sets itself up against the [true] knowledge of God, and we are taking every thought and purpose captive to the obedience of Christ, being ready to punish every act of disobedience, when your own obedience [as a church] is complete". 1 Corinthians 10:9-13; 2 Corinthians 10:4-6. AMP

Submit Your Total Being to God

To secure your joy, you **must** submit yourself to God.

"So, submit to [the authority of] God. Resist the devil [stand firm against him] and he will flee from you. Come close to God [with a contrite heart] and He will come close to you. Wash your hands, you sinners; and purify your [unfaithful] hearts, you double-minded [people]. Be miserable and grieve and weep [over your sin]. Let your [foolish] laughter be turned *to mourning and your [reckless] joy to gloom. Humble your-selves [with an attitude of repentance and insignificance] in the presence of the Lord, and He will exalt you [He will lift you up, He will give you purpose].*

Therefore, I urge you, brothers and sisters, by the mercies of God, to present your bodies [dedicating all of yourselves, set apart] as a living sacrifice, holy and well-pleasing to God, which is your rational (logical, intelligent) act of worship. And do not be conformed to this world [any longer with its su-perficial values and customs], but be transformed and progres-sively changed [as you mature spiritually] by the renewing of your mind [focusing on godly values and ethical attitudes], so that you may prove [for yourselves] what the will of God is, that which is good and acceptable and perfect [in His plan and pur-pose for you]". James 4:7-10; Romans 12:1-2. AMP

Walk in the Spirit

If you are really a child of God, you will not enjoy walking in the flesh, because walking in the flesh is not walking like Christ.

"Therefore, since we are surrounded by so great a cloud of witnesses [who by faith have testified to the truth of God's absolute faithfulness], stripping off every unnecessary weight and the sin which so easily and cleverly entangles us, let us run with endurance and active persistence the race that is set be-fore us, [looking away from all that will distract us and] focus-ing our eyes on Jesus, who is the Author and Perfecter of faith [the first incentive for our belief and the One who brings our faith to maturity], who for the joy [of accomplishing the goal] set before Him endured the cross, disregarding the shame, and sat down at the right hand of the throne of God [revealing His deity, His authority, and the completion of His work]. But I say, walk habitually in the Holy] Spirit [seek Him and be responsive to His guidance], and then you will certainly not carry out the desire of the sinful nature [which responds impulsively without regard for God and His precepts].

Now the practices of the sinful nature are clearly evident: they are sexual immorality, impurity, sensuality (total irresponsibility, lack of self-control), idolatry, sorcery, hostility, strife, jealousy, fits of anger, disputes, dissensions, factions [that promote heresies], envy, drunkenness, riotous behavior, and other things like these. I warn you beforehand, just as I did previously, that those who practice such things will not inherit the kingdom of God. But the fruit of the Spirit [the result of His presence within us] is love [unselfish concern for others], joy, [inner] peace, patience [not the ability to wait, but how we act while waiting], kindness, goodness, faithfulness, gentleness, self-control. Against such things there is no law. And those who belong to Christ Jesus have crucified the sinful nature together with its passions and appetites. If we [claim to] live by the [Holy] Spirit, we must also walk by the Spirit [with personal integrity, godly character, and moral courage—our conduct empowered by the Holy Spirit]".
Hebrews 12:1-2; Galatians 5: 16, 19-25. AMP

Think Like Christ and Be Anxious for Nothing

"For what person knows the thoughts and motives of a man except the man's spirit within him? So also no one knows the thoughts of God except the Spirit of God. Now we have received, not the spirit of the world, but the [Holy] Spirit who is from God, so that we may know and understand the [wonderful] things freely given to us by God. We also speak of these things, not in words taught or supplied by human wisdom, but in those taught by the Spirit, combining and interpreting spiritual thoughts with spiritual words [for those being guided by the Holy Spirit]. But the natural [unbelieving] man does not accept the things [the teachings and revelations] of the Spirit of God, for they are foolishness [absurd and illogical] to him; and he is incapable of understanding them, because they are spiritually discerned and appreciated, [and he is unqualified to judge spiritual matters].

But the spiritual man [the spiritually mature Christian] judges all things [questions, examines, and applies what the Holy Spirit reveals], yet is himself judged by no one [the unbeliever cannot judge and understand the believer's spiritual nature]. For who has known the mind and purposes of the Lord, so as to instruct Him? But we have the mind of Christ [to be guided by His thoughts and purposes]. Do not be anxious or worried about anything, but in everything [every circumstance and situation] by prayer and petition with thanksgiving, continue to make your [specific] requests known to God. And the peace of God [that peace which reassures the heart] which transcends all understanding, [that peace which] stands guard over your hearts and your minds in Christ Jesus [is yours]. Finally, believers, whatever is true, whatever is honorable and worthy of respect, whatever is right and confirmed by God's word, whatever is pure and wholesome, whatever is lovely and brings peace, whatever is admirable and of good repute; if there is any excellence, if there is anything worthy of praise, think continually on these things [center your mind on them, and implant them in your heart]". 1 Corinthians 2:11-16; Philippians 4:6-8. AMP

Feed Daily on God's Word and Prosper in Joy

"The law of the LORD is perfect (flawless), restoring and refreshing the soul; The statutes of the LORD are reliable and trustworthy, making wise the simple. The precepts of the LORD are right, bringing joy to the heart; The commandment of the LORD is pure, enlightening the eyes. The fear of the LORD is clean, enduring forever; The judgments of the LORD are true, they are righteous altogether. They are more desirable than gold, yes, than much fine gold; Sweeter also than honey and the drippings of the honeycomb. Moreover, by them Your servant is warned [reminded, illuminated, and instructed]; In keeping them there is great reward. All Scripture is God-breathed [given by divine inspiration] and is profitable for instruction, for conviction [of sin], for correction [of error and restoration

to obedience], for training in righteousness [learning to live in conformity to God's will, both publicly and privately—behaving honorably with personal integrity and moral courage]; so that the man of God may be complete and proficient, outfitted and thoroughly equipped for every good work.

Blessed [fortunate, prosperous, and favored by God] is the man who does not walk in the counsel of the wicked [following their advice and example], nor stand in the path of sinners, nor sit [down to rest] in the seat of scoffers (ridiculers). But his delight is in the law of the LORD, and on His law [His precepts and teachings] he [habitually] meditates day and night. And he will be like a tree firmly planted [and fed] by streams of water, which yields its fruit in its season; Its leaf does not wither; And in whatever he does, he prospers [and comes to maturity]." Psalm 19:7-11; 2 Timothy 3:16-17; Psalm 1: 1-3. AMP

Pray for Others

God encourages us to pray for others. When we pray for others in danger, in need, or under satanic attacks, we are sowing the seeds of joy, love, and peace for ourselves and our families. When we make the sacrifice of love, we will reap the miracles of love. One of the secrets to Job's restoration after been attacked severely by the devil from all corners was the prayer he prayed for his friends regardless of how they treated him in his time of need. Job needed prayers, love, and encouragement not criticism, been judged and degraded as a sinner who deserved what he wanted. God rebuked Job's friends as He will rebuke many of us, because we sometimes behave like Jobs friends when some of us are caught in an error or make mistakes. However, Job, in love reached out to his friends and prayed for them. Such prayers are like sowing in tears.

Nobody I know of is happy to passionately pray with all zeal and power for his or her enemies, haters, or persecutors, but we need to in love and in obedience to the Lord.

Job did and that was when he got the Divine assistance he needed. Job sowed in tears and reaped in joy. God paid him double for his pain, and turned his pain to gain.

"It came about that after the Lord had spoken these words to Job, that the Lord said to Eliphaz the Temanite, "My wrath is kindled against you and against your two friends, for you have not spoken of Me what is right, as My servant Job has. Now therefore, take for yourselves seven bulls and seven rams, and go to My servant Job, and offer up a burnt offering for yourselves, and My servant Job will pray for you. For I will accept him [and his prayer] so that I may not deal with you according to your folly, because you have not spoken of Me the thing that is right, as My servant Job has." So Eliphaz the Temanite and Bildad the Shuhite and Zophar the Naamathite went and did as the Lord told them; and the Lord accepted Job's prayer.

The Lord restored the fortunes of Job when he prayed for his friends, and the Lord gave Job twice as much as he had before. Then all his brothers and sisters and all who had known him before came to him, and they ate bread with him in his house; and they consoled him and comforted him over all the [distressing] adversities that the Lord had brought on him. And each one gave him a piece of money, and each a ring of gold. And the Lord blessed the latter days of Job more than his beginning; for he had 14,000 sheep, 6,000 camels, 1,000 yoke of oxen, and 1,000 female donkeys. He had seven sons and three daughters. And he called the name of the first [daughter] Jemimah, and the name of the second Keziah, and the name of the third Keren-happuch. In all the land there were found no women so fair as the daughters of Job; and their father gave them an inheritance among their brothers. After this, Job lived 140 years, and saw his sons and his grandsons, four generations". Job 42: 7-16. AMP

Chapter 11

The Levels of Joy

The Christian life is a life of growth in Christ, we are God's branches, attached to the God head through Jesus Christ. The more we grow in Christ's love and grace, the more we will grow into greater levels of joy. Increase in your joy means an increase in your spiritual strength and an increase of the peace in your soul. Increase in spiritual strength means an increase in your faith in Christ and your love for others. Increase in your faith and love for others means an increase in your spiritual power and more grace. The more grace you have, the more spiritual power you will have to resist the devil, overcome him, and enjoy the abundant life in Christ. Hence joy is the fruit of the Spirit, then it is true that we can grow from one level of joy to another, from saving joy into the joy of discipleship.

*"You have put **more joy and rejoicing in my heart** than [they know] when their wheat and new wine have yielded abundantly"*. Psalm 4: 7. AMPC

1. Joy of Faith

The greatest joy of all joy is the joy of salvation, greater than the joy of casting out demons, healing the sick, and even raising the dead back to life. Jesus Himself declares that we should rejoice in our salvation, and that our names are written in the book of life. The greatest miracle of all miracles is the miracle of salvation.

"The seventy returned with joy, saying, "Lord, even the demons are subject to us in Your name." He said to them, "I watched Satan fall from heaven like [a flash of] lightning. Listen carefully: I have given you authority [that you now possess] to tread on serpents and scorpions, and [the ability to exercise authority] over all the power of the enemy (Satan); and

*nothing will [in any way] harm you. Nevertheless, do not re-
joice at this, that the spirits are subject to you, but **rejoice that
your names are recorded in heaven.** "* Luke 10:17-20. AMP

The Joy of Faith Is Also the joy of Reconciliation
The apostle Paul was caught between two thoughts, choos-
ing to die or to live so he could continue to encourage the saints.
He too acknowledges the joy of faith. Jesus came to reconcile
us to God.

*"Therefore, since we have been justified [that is, acquitted
of sin, declared blameless before God] by faith, [let us grasp
the fact that] we have peace with God [and the joy of reconcil-
iation with Him] through our Lord Jesus Christ (the Messiah,
the Anointed). Since I am convinced of this, I know that I will
remain and continue with all of you for your progress and joy
in the faith, "*. Romans 5:1; Philippians 1: 25. AMP

2. Exceeding Joy
Exceeding joy is the gradual increase of joy from a mere
joy of comfort to a joy of being found in God and growing in
relationship with Jesus Christ our Lord. The blessing of becoming Spirit-filled.

*"His master said to him, 'Well done, good and faithful
servant. You have been faithful and trustworthy over a little, I
will put you in charge of many things; share in the joy of your
master.' Then I will go to the altar of God, to God, my
exceeding joy; With the lyre I will praise You, O God, my God!
Be glad and exceedingly joyful, for your reward in heaven is
great [absolutely inexhaustible]; for in this same way they persecuted the prophets who were before you"*. Matthew 25:21;
Psalm 43:4; Matthew 5:12. AMP

3. Abundant Joy
Abundant joy comes when you and I begin to discover who
we are in Christ, and gradually begin to learn how to exercise
our God given authority in Christ.

"And now, brothers and sisters, we want you to know about the grace God gave the churches in Macedonia. Although they have been tested by great troubles [trials; tribulation] and are very poor, they gave much because of their great joy [their deep poverty and abundant joy overflowed into rich generosity]. I can tell you [testify] that they gave as much as they were able and even more than they could afford. No one told them to do it". 2 Corinthians 8:1-3. EXB

4. Great Joy

Great joy comes when you learn to begin to accomplish great things for God. It is the joy of sacrificial living, the ability to honor the Lord with our lives. Great joy is the joy we experience when God uses us and we see souls saved, and criminals becoming saints. Great joy is the joy of becoming great temples of our great and loving God passionately.

"Then the people rejoiced over their freewill offerings because with a whole heart they offered willingly to Adonai. King David also rejoiced with great joy". 1 Chronicles 29:9. TLV

"Also on that day they offered great sacrifices and rejoiced because God had given them great joy; the women and children also rejoiced, so that the joy of Jerusalem was heard from far away. But insofar as you are sharing Christ's sufferings, keep on rejoicing, so that when His glory [filled with His radiance and splendor] is revealed, you may rejoice with great joy". Nehemiah 12:43; 1 Peter 4:13. AMP

5. Overflowing Joy

Overflowing joy is when we now begin to abide in Christ as His ambassadors or disciples, and used by the Lord to disciple others.

"If you keep My commandments [if you continue to obey My instructions], you will abide in My love and live on in it, just as I have obeyed My Father's commandments and live on in His love. I have told you these things, that My joy and delight may

be in you, and that your joy and gladness may be of full meas-
ure and complete and overflowing. I have great boldness and
   free and fearless confidence and cheerful courage toward
you; my pride in you is great. I am filled [brimful] with the com-
fort [of it]; with all our tribulation and in spite of it, [I am filled
with comfort] I am overflowing with joy." John 15:10-11;
2 Corinthians 7:4. AMPC

6. Glorious Joy

   Glorious joy is the joy of finishing well and strong, when
one rejoices in gaining eternal rest. Many started well but ended
bad. It is my prayer that you will finish well and strong, so you
will be granted access to eternal life and joy, in Jesus name.

   Therefore, since we are surrounded by so great a cloud of
witnesses [who by faith have testified to the truth of God's ab-
solute faithfulness], stripping off every unnecessary weight and
the sin which so easily and cleverly entangles us, let us run with
endurance and active persistence the race that is set before
us, [looking away from all that will distract us and] focusing
our eyes on Jesus, who is the Author and Perfecter of faith [the
first incentive for our belief and the One who brings our faith
to maturity], who for the joy [of accomplishing the goal] set
before Him endured the cross, disregarding the shame, and sat
down at the right hand of the throne of God [revealing His de-
ity, His authority, and the completion of His work].

   In this you rejoice greatly, even though now for a little
while, if necessary, you have been distressed by various tri-
als, so that the genuineness of your faith, which is much more
precious than gold which is perishable, even though
tested and purified by fire, may be found to result in [your]
praise and glory and honor at the revelation of Jesus
Christ. Though you have not seen Him, you love Him; and
though you do not even see Him now, you believe and trust in
Him and you greatly rejoice and delight with inexpressible and
glorious joy". It will be said in that day, "Indeed, this is our
God for whom we have waited that He would save us. This is the

Lord for whom we have waited; Let us shout for joy and re-
joice in His salvation". Hebrews 12:1-2;
1 Peter 1:6-8; Isaiah 25: 9. AMP

Some Ways Joy Was Expressed in the Bible
1. Shout of Joy

It is not a sin to shout for joy. We shout not because God is
deaf, but because He enjoys it, and we cannot hold back our
excitement for His great love and Almighty-ness. It is the win-
ning side that is the shouting side. So, please, go ahead and
praise God and shout for joy, for it is good to praise the Lord
for who He is and for all His wonderful benefits, especially for
our salvation.

"Now joy has gone away [or it (the plant) dissolves on the
way]; other plants grow up from the same dirt. "Surely God
does not reject the innocent or give strength to [or grasp the
hand of] those who do evil. God will yet fill your mouth with
laughter and your lips with shouts of joy. Your enemies [Those
who hate you] will be covered with shame, and the tents of the
wicked will be gone. It is good to praise [thank] you, Lord, to
sing praises to [make a psalm to the name of] God Most High.
It is good to tell of [proclaim] your love [loyalty] in the morn-
ing and of your loyalty [faithfulness] at night. It is good to
praise you with the ten-stringed lyre and with the soft-sounding
[melody of the] harp. Lord, you have made me happy
[rejoice] by what you have done; I will sing [shout] for joy
about what your hands have done [the works of your hand]".
Job 8: 19-22; Psalm 92:1-4. EXB

2. Singing for Joy

Singing and listening to worldly music makes one world-
lier, because what you feed the heart is what you become, and
what comes out of your heart is who you are on the inside. It's
been said that, when praises go up, blessings come down. We
often express our joy and gratitude to God by singing songs of
praise. If the unbelievers claim that music is the food of the soul,

78

then spirit-filled praise and worship is the energizer, healing balm, and refresher of the Christian soul.

"It shall blossom abundantly and rejoice even with joy and singing. The glory of Lebanon shall be given to it, the excellency of [Mount] Carmel and [the plain] of Sharon. They shall see the glory of the Lord, the majesty and splendor and excellency of our God". Isaiah 35: 2. AMP

3. Cry of Joy

You can sow in tears and reap in joy. I need not tell you the difference between the cry of joy and the cry of sorrow, shame, and reproach. If you have not experienced a miracle, you may not know what a cry of joy feels like. If you have not been given a few days, weeks, or months to live by the doctors and then God over-ruled the doctors report, you may not know how the cry of joy sounds like. If you have ever been through the valley of hopelessness, helplessness, and a disgraceful humiliation; and then God broke the chains, and changed your story; you will know what is it to cry the cry of joy.

"When the Lord brought back the captivity of Zion, we were like those who dream. Then our mouth was filled with laughter, and our tongue with singing. Then they said among the nations, "The Lord has done great things for them." The Lord has done great things for us, and we are glad. Bring back our captivity, O Lord, as the streams in the South. Those who sow in tears shall reap in joy. He who continually goes forth weeping, bearing seed for sowing, shall doubtless come again with rejoicing, bringing his sheaves with him". Psalm 126. NKJV

4. Jumping for Joy

Some people are too politically correct and **who is looking** at me minded; they feel too self-conscious to jump up and praise God. Those who have experienced God's faithfulness, mercy, and power will jump in adoration and thanksgiving to the Almighty God.

"But Peter said, "I don't have any silver or gold, but I do have something else I can give you. By the power of Jesus Christ from Nazareth—stand up and walk!" Then Peter took the man's right hand and lifted him up. Immediately his feet and legs became strong. He jumped up, stood on his feet, and began to walk. He went into the Temple area with them. He was walking and jumping and praising God. All the people recognized him. They knew he was the crippled man who always sat by the Beautiful Gate to beg for money. Now they saw this same man walking and praising God. They were amazed. They did not understand how this could happen. You can be happy then and jump for joy, because you have a great reward in heaven. The ancestors of those people did the same things to the prophets".
Acts 3:6-10; Luke 6:23. ERV

5. Dancing for Joy

If dancing in general is good for the body, you can imagine what dancing when praising God will do for your wellbeing. It is sad to see believers who would dance to worldly music in a heartbeat, but feel bored when others are busy dancing and praising God. It simply shows who they are on the inside and what is more important to them. Do you dance to gratify Satan, yourself, or to glorify God?

"Hallelujah! Sing to the Lord a new song, His praise in the assembly of the godly. Let Israel celebrate its Maker; let the children of Zion rejoice in their King. Let them praise His name with dancing and make music to Him with tambourine and lyre. Then the young woman will rejoice with dancing, while young and old men rejoice together. I will turn their mourning into joy, give them consolation, and bring happiness out of grief".
Psalm 149:1-3; Jeremiah 31:13. Holman HCSB

6. Celebration

It is my sincere prayer that the celebration of the Lord's goodness and faithfulness will not cease in your life, family, and home. That the enemies of joy will not have any cause to celebrate over you, in Jesus name. Whatever you have lost, from destiny helpers, if the enemy of joy has turned your helpers of destiny against you, or if any of your loved ones has wandered away. Today I come in agreement with you in prayer, that the Almighty God will restore all you have lost back to you physically or spiritually, in Jesus name. I don't need to tell you how to celebrate God, I suppose you should already know. When people mock you, write you off as unfruitful and a shame for them to identity with; then they laugh at you disgustingly with pride. And then God steps in and prove them wrong, now they are the ones begging for your help, you will not need anybody to show you how to celebrate the goodness of God.

"So, he got up and came to his father. But while he was still a long way off, his father saw him and was moved with compassion for him, and ran and embraced him and kissed him. And the son said to him, 'Father, I have sinned against heaven and in your sight; I am no longer worthy to be called your son.' But the father said to his servants, 'Quickly bring out the best robe [for the guest of honor] and put it on him; and give him a ring for his hand, and sandals for his feet. And bring the fattened calf and slaughter it, and let us [invite everyone and] feast and celebrate; for this son of mine was [as good as] dead and is alive again; he was lost and has been found.' So, they began to celebrate". Luke 15:20-24. AMP

Chapter 12

God Wants Your Life to Be Filled with Joy

"Instead of your [former] shame you will have a double portion; And instead of humiliation your people will shout for joy over their portion. Therefore, in their land they will possess double [what they had forfeited]; Everlasting joy will be theirs". Isaiah 61:7. AMP

The Devil Will Fight to Kill Your Joy, Don't Let Him

Jesus Christ went through pain and suffering, anguish, and humiliation, and then a cruel and horrific death on the Cross of Calvary so you and I can have life and have it more abundantly. All you and I need to do is to be willing to surrender our lives to Jesus, just like He Himself did at the garden of Gethsemane, when He cried out in humility and meekness, "Not My Will, Your Will Be Done".

"Then He said to them, "My soul is deeply grieved, so that I am almost dying of sorrow. Stay here and stay awake and keep watch with Me." And after going a little farther, He fell face down and prayed, saying, "My Father, if it is possible [that is, consistent with Your will], let this cup pass from Me; yet not as I will, but as You will." And He came to the disciples and found them sleeping, and said to Peter, "So, you men could not stay awake and keep watch with Me for one hour? Keep actively watching and praying that you may not come into temptation; the spirit is willing, but the body is weak." He went away a second time and prayed, saying, "My Father, if this cannot pass away unless I drink it, Your will be done"". Matthew 26:38-42. AMP

Trade in Your Sorrows for His Joy

What a blessing it is for us to be able to gain direct access to God the Father through Jesus Christ any time, any day, and any place with ease. Studying the book of Leviticus made me give glory to God for Jesus' sacrifice again and again. Jesus alone paid in full for our sins, all the sacrifices for different things in the book of Leviticus we don't have to do no more. All we got to do is let go, hand over our lives into Jesus' care, and let Him take over and make all things beautiful for us in His time. When we completely commit, yield ourselves, and truly focus on Jesus Christ in obedience; we will see the glory of God, and the devil will be in big trouble in our hands. Jesus Christ took our place on the Cross of Calvary. When Jesus died, He gave us the opportunity to be able to trade in our sorrows and shame, reproach and fear; sicknesses and diseases; for His overflowing joy, peace, glory and loving-kindness.

"Come now, and let us reason together," Says the Lord. "Though your sins are like scarlet, they shall be as white as snow; though they are red like crimson, they shall be like wool." If you are willing and obedient, you shall eat the best of the land; and My people, who are called by My Name, humble themselves, and pray and seek (crave, require as a necessity) My face and turn from their wicked ways, then I will hear [them] from heaven, and forgive their sin and heal their land." Isaiah 1:18-19; 2 Chronicles 7:14. AMP

No Matter What You Are Going through, Trust God

"Take your stand, indolent women! Listen to me! Indulgent, indolent women, listen closely to what I have to say. In just a little over a year from now, you'll be shaken out of your lazy lives. The grape harvest will fail, and there'll be no fruit on the trees. Oh tremble, you indolent women. Get serious, you pampered dolls! Strip down and discard your silk fineries. Put on funeral clothes. Shed honest tears for the lost harvest, the failed vintage. Weep for my people's gardens and farms that grow nothing but thistles and thorn-bushes.

Cry tears, real tears, for the happy homes no longer happy, the merry city no longer merry. The royal palace is deserted, the bustling city quiet as a morgue, the emptied parks and playgrounds taken over by wild animals, delighted with their new

home. Yes, weep and grieve until the Spirit is poured down on us from above, and the badlands desert grows crops, and the fertile fields become forests. Justice will move into the badlands desert. Right will build a home in the fertile field and where there's Right, there'll be Peace and the progeny of Right: quiet lives and endless trust. My people will live in a peaceful neighborhood—in safe houses, in quiet gardens. The forest of your pride will be clear-cut, the city showing off your power leveled. But you will enjoy a blessed life, planting well-watered fields and gardens, with your farm animals grazing freely".
Isaiah 32:13-20. MSG

Jesus is the Answer that You Need

Drugs are not the answer, they will not make your problems go away. Alcohol is not the answer, it will impair your judgment and it is also dangerous to your health. Prostitution or excessive sex will not help, it leads to all kinds of diseases. Suicide is not the answer, God considers it murder, why should you destroy your life when there is hope for you in Christ. Jesus is the healer when you are sick. Jesus is the master of the storm, He will calm your storm if you will let Him. Jesus is the way when you are confused and lost. When you are hopeless, helpless, and in trouble, that is not the time to run away from God, it is the best time to run to Him, so He can give you beauty for your ashes, and make all things beautiful for you for His glory.

When life is tough and hard on you, it is not the time to run away from those who love you, it is the time for soul searching, and a time to get right with God. God will never turn His back on you if you are seeking His forgiveness. God is always willing to help us, but we often let our pride get in the way. God's hands and arms are always stretched out, open wide to receive us back. It doesn't matter the amount sins you may have committed, God is willing and ready to forgive, if you can just humble yourself and ask for His help, forgiveness, and mercy. God is ready, if you are willing, if you are ready to take the first step. Open your heart and mouth, tell Him you are ready. Pray to

84

Him, ask for His forgiveness and accept Jesus into your life as your Lord and personal savior. If you pray that prayer, it is that simple, Jesus will come into your life, you will experience the river of joy flowing subtly and calmly into your soul.

Jesus is life, if you don't have Jesus, you will never know real peace and joy. Any life without Jesus is hardly free of crisis. Jesus is the master of all storms, the peace and hope amid any storm we will ever go through in life. Put your trust in Jesus, rest on the wings of His power, and let Him ride you out of any storm you are in. Congratulations on your salvation, I rejoice with you if you have made Jesus Christ your Lord and savior, receiving Jesus Christ into your life may be the best decision of your life.

"For God, so [greatly] loved and dearly prized the world, that He [even] gave His [One and] only begotten Son, so that whoever believes and trusts in Him [as Savior] shall not perish, but have eternal life. For God did not send the Son into the world to judge and condemn the world [that is, to initiate the final judgment of the world], but that the world might be saved through Him. Whoever believes and has decided to trust in Him [as personal Savior and Lord] is not judged [for this one, there is no judgment, no rejection, no condemnation]; but the one who does not believe [and has decided to reject Him as personal Savior and Lord] is judged already [that one has been convicted and sentenced], because he has not believed and trusted in the name of the [One and] only begotten Son of God [the One who is truly unique, the only One of His kind, the One who alone can save him].

The thief comes only in order to steal and kill and destroy. I came that they may have and enjoy life, and have it in abundance [to the full, till it overflows]. I am the Good Shepherd. The Good Shepherd lays down His [own] life for the sheep. But the hired man [who merely serves for wages], who is neither the shepherd nor the owner of the sheep, when he sees the wolf

coming, deserts the flock and runs away; and the wolf snatches the sheep and scatters them. The man runs because he is a hired hand [who serves only for wages] and is not concerned about the [safety of the] sheep. I am the Good Shepherd, and I know [without any doubt those who are] My own and My own know Me [and have a deep, personal relationship with Me]— even as the Father knows Me and I know the Father—and I lay down My [very own] life [sacrificing it] for the benefit of the sheep. "Come to Me, all who are weary and heavily burdened [by religious rituals that provide no peace], and I will give you rest [refreshing your souls with salvation]".
John 3:16-18; 10:10-15; Matthew 11:28. AMP

Rest in God's Word and You Will Have Joy

"For as the rain and snow come down from heaven, and do not return there without watering the earth, making it bear and sprout, and providing seed to the sower and bread to the eater, so will My word be which goes out of My mouth; It will not return to Me void (useless, without result), without accomplishing what I desire, and without succeeding in the matter for which I sent it. The law of the Lord is perfect (flawless), restoring and refreshing the soul; The statutes of the Lord are reliable and trustworthy, making wise the simple. The precepts of the Lord are right, bringing joy to the heart; The commandment of the Lord is pure, enlightening the eyes. The fear of the Lord is clean, enduring forever; The judgments of the Lord are true, they are righteous altogether. They are more desirable than gold, yes, than much fine gold; Sweeter also than honey and the drippings of the honeycomb. Moreover, by them Your servant is warned [reminded, illuminated, and instructed]; In keeping them there is great reward." Psalm 19:7-11;
Isaiah 55:10-11. AMP

Eternal Joy Is the Dream of Every Christian

Heaven is full of joy. If you can make it there, joy will be yours forever. Jesus Christ our Lord ascended to prepare a place for you and me in heaven, and He is coming back with rewards for those who have and are continuing to serve Him in spirit and in truth.

"His master said to him, 'Well done, good and faithful servant. You have been faithful and trustworthy over a little, I will put you in charge of many things; share in the joy of your master'. Do not let your heart be troubled (afraid, cowardly). Believe [confidently]in God and trust in Him, [have faith, hold on to it, rely on it, keep going and] believe also in Me. In My Father's house are many dwelling places. If it were not so, I would have told you, because I am going there to prepare a place for you. And if I go and prepare a place for you, I will come back again and I will take you to Myself, so that where I am you may be also". Matthew 25: 21; John 14: 1-3 AMP

You Are Safe in God's Hands

"He who dwells in the shelter of the Most High will remain secure and rest in the shadow of the Almighty [whose power no enemy can withstand]. I will say of the Lord, "He is my refuge and my fortress, My God, in whom I trust [with great confidence, and on whom I rely]!" For He will save you from the trap of the fowler, and from the deadly pestilence. He will cover you and completely protect you with His pinions, and under His wings you will find refuge; His faithfulness is a shield and a wall. You will not be afraid of the terror of night, nor of the arrow that flies by day, nor of the pestilence that stalks in darkness, nor of the destruction (sudden death) that lays waste at noon. A thousand may fall at your side and ten thousand at your right hand, but danger will not come near you. You will only [be a spectator as you] look on with your eyes and witness the [divine] repayment of the wicked [as you watch safely from the shelter of the Most-High]. Because you have made the Lord, [who is] my refuge, even the Most-High, your dwelling place, no evil will befall you, nor will any plague come near your tent.

For He will command His angels in regard to you, to protect and defend and guard you in all your ways [of obedience and service]. They will lift you up in their hands, so that you do

not [even] strike your foot against a stone. You will tread upon the lion and cobra; The young lion and the serpent you will trample underfoot. "Because he set his love on Me, therefore I will save him; I will set him [securely] on high, because he knows My name [he confidently trusts and relies on Me, knowing I will never abandon him, no, never]. "He will call upon Me, and I will answer him; I will be with him in trouble; I will rescue him and honor him. "With a long life, I will satisfy him and I will let him see My salvation."" Psalm 91. AMP

My Prayer for You

"And this I pray, that your love may abound more and more [displaying itself in greater depth] in real knowledge and in practical insight, so that you may learn to recognize and treasure what is excellent [identifying the best, and distinguishing moral differences], and that you may be pure and blameless until the day of Christ [actually living lives that lead others away from sin]; filled with the fruit of righteousness which comes through Jesus Christ, to the glory and praise of God [so that His glory may be both revealed and recognized].

May the God of hope fill you with all joy and peace in believing [through the experience of your faith] that by the power of the Holy Spirit you will abound in hope and overflow with confidence in His promises. So that you will walk in a manner worthy of the Lord [displaying admirable character, moral courage, and personal integrity], to [fully] please Him in all things, bearing fruit in every good work and steadily growing in the knowledge of God [with deeper faith, clearer insight and fervent love for His precepts]; [we pray that you may be] strengthened and invigorated with all power, according to His glorious might, to attain every kind of endurance and patience with joy; giving thanks to the Father, who has qualified us to share in the inheritance of the saints (God's people) in the Light." Philippians 1: 9-11; Romans 15:13; Colossians 1: 10-12. AMP

Author Information

Pastor Joseph Blessing Omosigho is a full gospel preacher and teacher of the living Word of God. To order books, or make an invitation to Pastor Joseph, please call, write, or email us at the address below:

Angels on Assignment
2013 Wellington Point, Heartland, Texas 75126
Tel: 214-994-8080
Email: ministryofchrist@gmail.com

Other Books Written by Pastor Joseph Blessing Omosigho:
1. Knocked Down But Not Knocked Out
2. Your Phone Connection Versus Your Prayer Connection
3. Woman, Build Your Home or Destroy It
4. Pastors and Church Leaders Con Games
5. Leading God's Way
6. Don't Give Up, Dream Again
7. It Pays to Wait on God
8. God Still Speaks
9. What the Church is and is Not
10. Anger, Manage it or Blow it

The Enemies of Joy; Please, don't allow anyone or anything to steal your Joy. It is my prayer that the enemies of joy will not prevail against you, to steal, kill, or destroy (shatter) your joy, in Jesus name. Jesus loves you and so do I!

"Finally, brethren, farewell (rejoice)! Be strengthened (perfected, completed, made what you ought to be); be encouraged and consoled and comforted; be of the same [agreeable] mind one with another; live in peace, and [then] the God of love [Who is the Source of affection, goodwill, love, and benevolence toward men] and the Author and Promoter of peace will be with you". 2 Corinthians 13:11 AMP

Made in the USA
Middletown, DE
18 August 2022